THE CENTRE FOR ENTERPRISE, MARKETS AND ETHICS

ENTERPRISE AND VALUES SERIES

THE UK SAVINGS CRISIS
REDISCOVERING THE PRINCIPLE AND PRACTICE OF SAVING

ANDREI ROGOBETE

First Edition, 2020

ISBN: 978-1-910666-19-7

Published by:
Centre for Enterprise, Markets and Ethics, 31 Beaumont Street, Oxford OX1 2NP

Design by Push Start Marketing Ltd, 46 Market Square, Witney, Oxfordshire OX28 6AL

Printed in the United Kingdom by Foremost Print Ltd, Unit 9a, Vantage Business Park, Bloxham Road, Banbury, Oxfordshire OX16 9UX

The Centre for Enterprise, Markets and Ethics

We are a think tank based in Oxford that seeks to promote an enterprise, market economy built on ethical foundations.

We undertake research on the interface of Christian theology, economics and business.

Our aim is to argue the case for an economy that generates wealth, employment, innovation and enterprise within a framework of calling, integrity, values and ethical behaviour, leading to the transformation of the business enterprise and contributing to the relief of poverty.

We publish a range of material, hold events and conferences, undertake research projects and speak and teach in our areas of concern.

We are independent and a registered charity entirely dependent on donations for our work.

Our website is www.theceme.org.

For further information please contact the Director, Richard Turnbull, at:

The Centre for Enterprise, Markets and Ethics
First Floor, 31 Beaumont Street,
Oxford OX1 2NP

ABOUT THE AUTHOR

Andrei E. Rogobete is Associate Director with the Centre for Enterprise, Markets and Ethics. He is the author of several publications, including *Ethics in Global Business: Building Moral Capitalism* and *The Challenges of Migration*. His main areas of research include business ethics, sustainable governance, as well as the contemporary role of Judeo-Christian teaching. He also writes regularly on the wider socio-economic challenges facing Britain and the western world.

Andrei's background is in political consulting and media relations, having previously worked in Westminster for Media Intelligence Partners (MIP). During his time at MIP, he worked on bespoke political campaigns for several high-profile politicians and members of the Cabinet.

He holds an MSc from University College London in Business and a BA in Politics and International Relations from Royal Holloway, University of London, together with a Certificate in Theological Studies from the University of Oxford.

CONTENTS

Introduction

Over one-third of people in Britain have less than £1,500 in savings and 15 per cent have no savings at all.[1] Young people are the most affected group: an estimated 53 per cent of 22–29-year-olds have zero savings.[2] The House of Commons Treasury Committee estimates that over 75 per cent of 25–34-year-olds do not own any form of residential property.[3] In addition, the cuts in interest rates – to as low as 0.01 per cent in 2020 on savings accounts – have acted as a further disincentive to save.[4]

Against the backdrop of Brexit and Covid-19, this is a good time to set the economic and social foundations for Britain in the rest of the twenty-first century. The country needs to rediscover the virtues of prudence and stewardship in an increasingly complex environment in which a culture of consumerism, or 'Buy now, pay later', seems the norm.

The economic growth of the last decade has not benefited everyone equally, leaving some in difficult financial circumstances. The economic ghosts of the recession linger: lagging productivity; slow income growth; declining home ownership; low interest rates. These factors amount to a difficult environment for saving.

In a recent interview, the former Governor of the Bank of England, Mervyn King, said:

> We have not been looking at the underlying economic challenges for the United Kingdom. We have one of the lowest saving rates in the British economy of any G20 country. We're not saving enough for pensions, we're not saving enough to care for the elderly, we're not saving enough for infrastructure. What are we going to do about the education of 50 per cent of the population that don't go to university or college? These are the issues that will determine our prosperity in the future.[5]

Technology is also changing the way we use money. The 'Access to Cash' Review commissioned in 2018 found that the UK could become a cashless society in only 15 years. A decade ago, 6 out of 10 transactions were made with cash; today it is 3 out of 10. Britain's cashless transition would leave an estimated 8 million people who rely on cash struggling financially.[6]

Yet beyond our gradual move away from cash lie the associated difficulties and confusion of an increasingly complex spending system. The lines between what people hold as traditional 'cash in the bank' and what they can spend are blurred. More recent trends that merge activities such as shopping with previously separate ones such as entertainment and social time only add to the budgetary confusion. In such a context, financial literacy becomes essential if people are to avoid the pitfalls that come with heightened complexity.

'Britain needs to rediscover the culture and habit of saving'

Thus Britain needs to rediscover the culture and habit of saving. The purpose of this publication is twofold: first, to understand the causes of the current savings crisis and discuss some of the initiatives and measures that can be used to combat it; second, to discover how the virtue of prudence contributes to recognising the principle and practice of saving as central to the long-term socio-economic health and development of British society.

Chapter 1 looks at the economic situation in the UK and the key aspects of its low level of savings. It considers some of the predominant underlying economic and demographic issues that have made it difficult for people to save. The chapter also briefly surveys some of the theories associated with predicting future levels of savings, such as the Permanent Income Hypothesis and the Life Cycle of Consumption Hypothesis. It also evaluates current initiatives in three main areas: emergency savings; savings for a first home; savings for retirement.

Chapter 2 focuses on the historical use of money and the moral arguments for saving. It considers human nature within classical thought and presents Adam Smith's defence of prudence as one of the key virtues necessary to develop a culture of saving. The chapter concludes with a brief exploration of prudence within Judeo-Christian teaching, and argues that it is an integral part of human and spiritual flourishing.

Chapter 3 draws some conclusions and includes suggestions for further action. It argues that the UK's low levels of savings can be alleviated if changes take place in key areas: creating an environment that rewards saving; broadening asset ownership; reforming intra-generational equity; rediscovering the virtue of prudence in establishing a culture of saving, in particular promoting financial education.

NOTES TO INTRODUCTION

1   Charlie Barton, 'Saving Statistics', Finder.com, 20 August 2019; https://www.finder.com/uk/saving-statistics.
2   Ibid.
3   House of Commons Treasury Committee, 'Household Finances: Income, Saving and Debt; Nineteenth Report of Session 2017–19', p. 6.
4   David Byers, 'NS&I Rates: Big Squeeze hits 25m Savers and Premium Bond Holders', *The Times*, 22 September 2020, https://www.thetimes.co.uk/article/ns-amp-i-rates-big-squeeze-hits-25m-savers-and-premium-bond-holders-r56jb0bfq.
5   Andy Gregory, 'Brexit Stopping Britain Resolving Deep Problems with Economy, says former Bank of England Chief', *The Independent*, 20 October 2019; https://www.independent.co.uk/news/uk/politics/brexit-economy-mervyn-king-bank-england-election-recession-debt-a9163531.html.
6   Access to Cash Review – Final Report, March 2019; https://www.accesstocash.org.uk/media/1087/final-report-final-web.pdf.

Chapter 1

The UK savings crisis

1.1 The potential impact of Covid-19

First, the elephant in the room. The lockdown brought on by Covid-19 has had a profound impact on social and economic life in Britain. It has brought the wheels of the economy to an abrupt standstill. However, the lockdown was *imposed* – the economic activity downturn was not the result of a macro issue in the economy or the bursting of an overinflated market bubble. Economic activity in Britain has been shut down forcefully for the first time since the Second World War.

What will be the likely impact of the lockdown on savings? Will it exacerbate the discrepancy between the haves and have-nots? How quick could a recovery be? These are just a few of the questions that require answers.

Two likely outcomes

The biotech entrepreneur and social impact investor Dato Dr Kim Tan recently wrote in a report:

> Whoever said that Covid-19 is the great equalizer was wrong. We may be in the same storm, but we are definitely not all in the same boat. Covid-19 is widening inequalities. The poor will be hit the hardest by this pandemic.[1]

The most likely and unfortunate outcome of the lockdown will be a growing discrepancy between haves and have-nots: those fortunate enough – and those unable – to maintain a steady income.

For those able to maintain income, the lockdown has had a positive impact on saving. A report from Legal & General estimates that spending has decreased by around £18 billion per month in the wider economy since lockdown began, effectively decreasing household spending by over one-third.[2] *The Telegraph* reports that savings deposits were up by £13 billion in March alone.[3] Nigel Green, the CEO and founder of the financial consulting firm deVere, recently argued:

> The financial impact of coronavirus has driven home that the 'living for today' attitude is great, but what happens when tomorrow does come? Are you still able to fulfil your obligations? Are you still able to do the things you love with your friends and family? Are you able to maintain your lifestyle? The crisis will, again, underscore that we're increasingly living in an era of personal financial responsibility. The pandemic has brought savings back into sharp focus.[4]

It may well be that the impact of Covid-19 will be far more profound than just a transitory reduction in spending. The crisis could prompt a holistic change in attitude towards spending that will last long after the pandemic has passed. Households may become more conservative and forward-looking in their discretionary spending. So those who have maintained employment are more likely to have increased their savings and therefore be in an overall healthier financial position.

However, for those unable to receive or maintain a steady stream of income, the lockdown has had a negative impact. This could be due to the nature of their work (e.g. unable to work from home), unemployment (caused by layoffs), an abrupt and dramatic reduction in business demand, and would include those job seeking or laid off prior to the lockdown.

A report by the Resolution Foundation found that households with low income are twice as likely as those with higher income to fund the lockdown with debt. The average savings for those in shut-down parts of the economy between March and June were £1,900 compared to £4,700 for those able to work from home.[5] According to the economist George Bangham, 'These wealth divides have been exposed by the crisis. While higher-income households have built up their savings, many lower-income households have run theirs down and had to turn to high-interest credit.'[6]

'Wealth divides have been exposed by the crisis'

In summary, the long-term effect of the lockdown will probably be to increase the discrepancy between those who have and those who have not been able to maintain a steady income. Time will tell how lasting these effects will be on overall household savings. For now, it is important to emphasise the worrying impact the lockdown has had on low-income households and those out of work.

1.2   THE UNDERLYING CAUSES

Between the economic crisis of 2007–8 and the Covid-19 pandemic, the UK's economy grew by an average of just under 2 per cent per year.[7] Yet so far as savings are concerned, any beneficial effects have not materialised on the ground. As mentioned in the Introduction, one-third of Britons have under £1,500 in savings and 15 per cent have none[8] (and among those aged 22–29 that rises to over 50 per cent[9]). A report published by Theos found that 16 million British people have less than £100 in savings.[10] However, before delving deeper into these statistics we must consider the wider economic and demographic structural problems that have created a difficult environment for saving, both as principle and habit:

- Slow income growth;
- Lagging productivity;
- Declining home ownership;
- An ageing population;
- Low interest rates.

Slow income growth

Over the last decade, the UK's GDP has experienced moderate but positive growth. The exception of course was 2008–9, when the economy shrank by some 4.5 per cent, although since then GDP has grown on average by 1.9 per cent per year.[11] However, as Figure 1.1 shows, this trend has not been followed in real-wage growth.

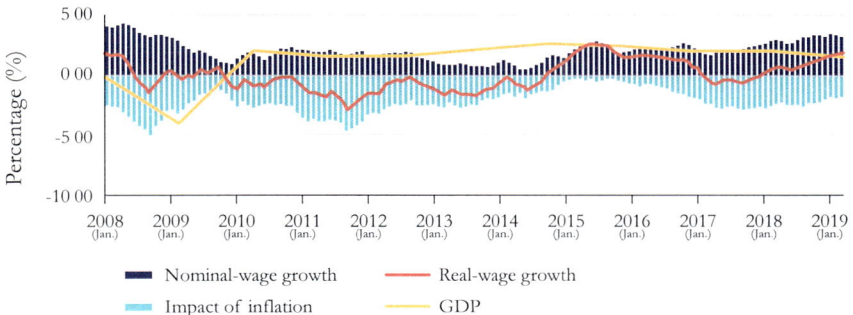

FIGURE 1.1: UK REAL WAGES VS GDP GROWTH

For the working population, the real-wage growth line points to a more volatile trajectory in the level of income. From the beginning of 2010 towards the end of 2015, any increase in wages has been more than cancelled out by inflation, resulting in a net negative change in real income. This can also be seen occurring in parts of 2008 and 2017. The picture for 2018–19 seems to be on a more positive trend, with real-wage growth standing at around 2 per cent in January 2019. The Office for National Statistics (ONS) estimates that other economic factors played a role in this, including: an increase in the employment rate from 75.6 per cent to 76.1 per cent; an increase in the tax-free Personal Allowance from £11,500 to £11,850; a pushback in the 40 per cent higher income tax rate for those earning above £45,000 per year to £46,350.[12]

However, what is key is the contrast between positive GDP growth and predominantly negative real-wage growth in the period 2010–14. This could help explain why the growth in the UK's economy over the last decade has not been felt in people's pockets.

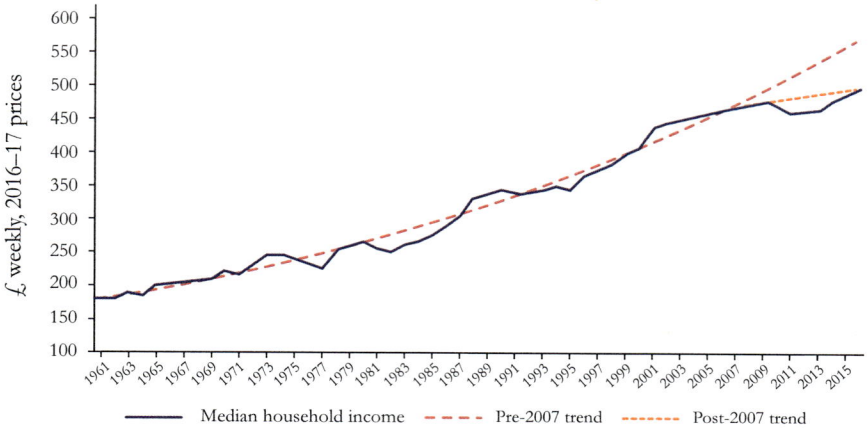

FIGURE 1.2: UK MEDIAN EQUIVALISED NET HOUSEHOLD INCOME

Digging a little deeper into the numbers, more worrying macro trends emerge. Figure 1.2 illustrates long-term growth in household income. There is a sudden change in the median income trend following the financial crises, albeit with some restoration around 2014. From the early 1970s to 2007, household incomes grew by an average of 2 per cent per year. After 2007, this dropped to just 0.6 per cent.[13] During a Parliamentary inquiry, Torsten Bell, the Director of the Resolution Foundation, told the House of Commons Treasury Committee that '[the effect on incomes of] the earnings squeeze that start[ed] to some degree in the mid-2000s and then became very severe from 2009 to 2014 ... is very big, and it dominates almost everything else.'[14]

Lagging productivity

Much like wage growth, UK productivity has also been lagging: despite a growing GDP, it stands among the bottom of the G7 countries, ahead only of Italy and 16.3 per cent lower than the G7 average.[15] Germany, France and the USA are more productive by 35, 30 and 20 per cent respectively. This means, for instance, that a French worker can produce by Thursday what a British worker cannot produce in the whole working week. The last time Britain claimed the top spot for European productivity was in 1960.[16]

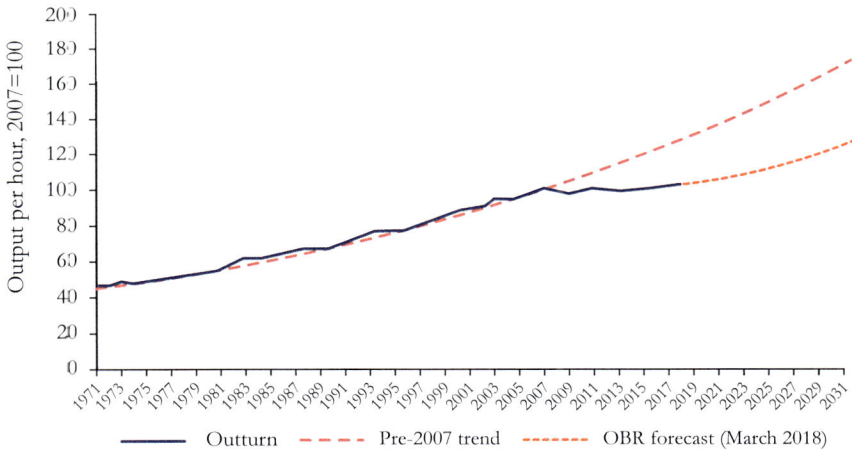

FIGURE 1.3: UK PRODUCTIVITY

Figure 1.3 illustrates the long-term trends in UK productivity growth. What appears clear is that the financial crisis of 2008 has had a significant impact not only on the initial growth trend but also on the UK's ability to return fully to its pre-crisis productivity growth trajectory. Even the prediction made by the Office for Budget Responsibility (OBR) sets productivity growth at 'roughly halfway between the pre-crisis (2 per cent) and post-crisis (0.5 per cent) averages'.[17] The 'productivity gap', which economists often refer to as the 'productivity puzzle', remains one of the most pressing issues for the British economy, and a direct contributor to low levels of household savings. Of course, the metrics are all interlinked, but the productivity puzzle has often been associated with: low capital investment; ageing technologies; limited bank lending; enduring skills shortages; poor levels of innovation. This all translates into a difficult environment for saving.

Declining home ownership

Home ownership in the UK has been on a downward trend since the early to mid-2000s. It reached a peak in 2002, when 58 per cent of all homes were owner-occupied, but by 2017 this had dropped to 51 per cent (with or without mortgages).[18]

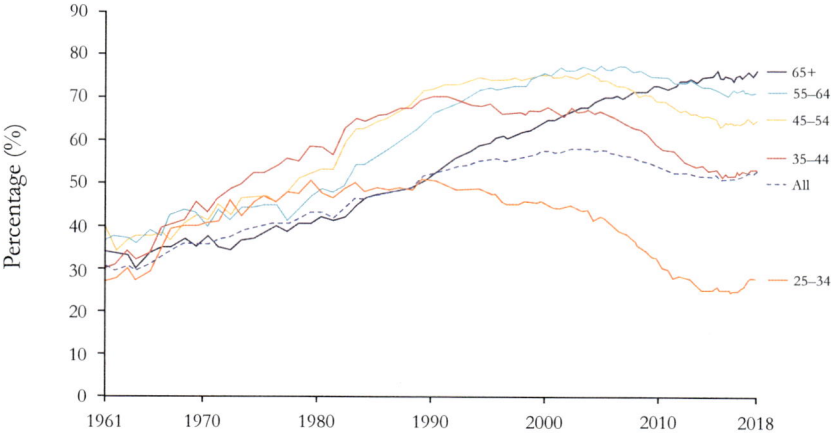

FIGURE 1.4: UK PERCENTAGE OWNING OWN HOME BY AGE GROUP

The more pertinent statistic, however, is home ownership trends among different age groups. Figure 1.4 illustrates how the turn of the century marked a downward trajectory for all age groups except

18

one: those 65 and older. The youngest age group (25–34-year-olds) has been the worst affected – and by a very large margin. If in 1990 around 50.5 per cent of all 25–34-year-olds were homeowners, by 2016 just 24.5 per cent were – a historic record low.

'The savings/home-ownership dynamic can rapidly turn into a vicious cycle'

Again, it is not just the youngest adults in society who are finding it difficult to afford a home – all age groups except those above 65 are facing similar struggles, albeit to varying degrees.

This is deeply concerning not just from an economic standpoint but because it strains the social fabric of British society for future generations. It can be seen as both a symptom and a cause of low levels of saving. Unable to purchase property due to lack of savings, many are, conversely, unable to build savings due to lack of – or poorly managed – income. The House of Commons Treasury Committee found that: 'If today's younger households continue to experience a reduced rate of home ownership through their lives, more of them will need to finance rent payments out of their retirement savings.'[19] The savings/home-ownership dynamic can rapidly turn into a vicious cycle with significant consequences down the road.

An ageing population

This data is straightforward: the British population is getting older. However, while the numbers may appear simple, the implications are not. Table 1.1 shows the latest ONS statistics and predictions of population growth by age groups.

The only demographic predicted to increase their share of the total population are those aged 60 and older. However, the population as a whole is predicted to increase from roughly 65 million in 2016 to 76 million by 2046, due primarily to two factors: an improvement in life expectancy; positive net migration. Data from the World Bank set life expectancy in the UK at 80.96 years in 2016 compared to 71.97 in 1970;[20] and more people are entering the UK than leaving, with a positive net migration average of 113,000 per year since 1975.[21]

Interestingly, an ageing population and positive net migration have clearly offset any decline or slowdown in the total population caused by falling birth rates. In 1965 there were 2.9 births per woman, while by 2016 this number had dropped to 1.8.[22]

So how does an ageing population have an impact on savings? The answer is: indirectly. The ONS considered some 'consequences' of the UK's ageing population, chief among which was a reduction in the number of those at working age alongside an increase in the number at pensionable age.[23] This not only places pressure on the national economy but raises questions around the sustainability of adequate provision of healthcare, housing and education.[24] In a report published by the Government Office for Science, Professor Sarah Harper notes that: 'Responding to this demographic shift will require us to make adaptations across many aspects of our lives: how we work; how we care for, communicate, and interact with each other.'[25]

	0–15 years (%)	16–64 years (%)	65+ years (%)	UK Population
1976	24.5	61.2	14.2	56,216,121
1986	20.5	64.1	15.4	56,683,835
1996	20.7	63.5	15.9	58,164,374
2006	19.2	64.9	15.9	60,827,067
2016	18.9	63.1	18.0	65,648,054
2026	18.8	60.7	20.5	69,843,515
2036	18.0	58.2	23.9	73,360,907
2046	17.7	57.7	24.7	76,342,235

TABLE 1.1: UK POPULATION, AGE DISTRIBUTION, PROJECTED TO 2046

Low interest rates

Following the 2008 financial crisis, the UK's bank rate has been maintained at historic lows, standing at 0.75 per cent in October 2019.[26] The Covid crisis has led to further reductions, seeing the rate reach 0.1 per cent in July 2020. Low interest rates create a difficult environment for saving – they are broadly intended to promote spending, not saving. It has therefore become cheaper – and more profitable –

'It is simply too expensive to put money aside'

to borrow than to save. Figure 1.5 illustrates the drop in the bank rate set by the Bank of England. It stood at a record high of 17 per cent in November 1979, an initial measure of the incoming Conservative government under Margaret Thatcher to combat inflation. In August 2016 it dropped to a record low of 0.25 per cent, to stimulate spending.

The current low-interest environment makes it difficult to build long-term savings – it is simply too expensive to put money aside when inflation hovers around 2 per cent and most standard retail bank accounts offer less than 1 per cent APR. This is ignoring, of course, the promotional-type savings accounts that promise higher interest rates only to default back to a low rate after a certain period (usually 12 months).[27]

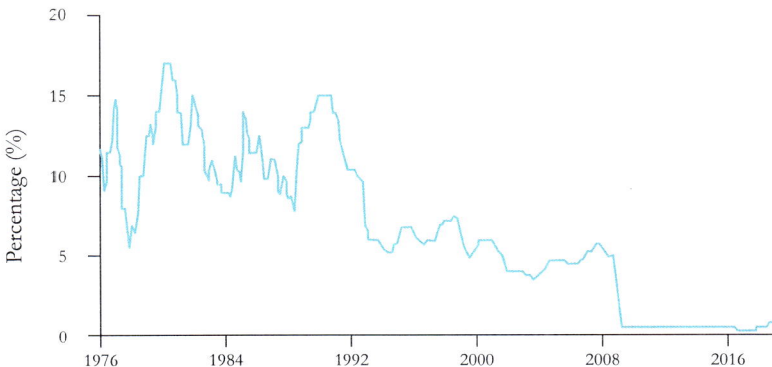

FIGURE 1.5: UK BANK RATE

Low interest rates incentivise not saving but either borrowing or the pursuit of higher-risk/higher-reward investments. In written evidence to the House of Commons Treasury Committee, the Financial Services Consumer Panel said that 'Saving [needs] to be seen in the context of a seemingly permanent low interest rate environment ... it is difficult and unrewarding to save.'[28]

1.3   THE PROBLEM ITSELF – HOW BIG IS IT?

Current statistics

To recap: five macro conditions are placing negative stress on saving (slow income growth; lagging productivity; declining home ownership; an ageing population; low interest rates); and current savings statistics paint a dark picture (almost one-third of UK adults with under £1,500 in savings;[29] 53 per cent of 22–29-year-olds with none;[30] 60 per cent of those earning under £13,000 p.a. ditto[31]).

The situation isn't much better in the USA. The 2019 Schwab Modern Wealth Survey found that of the 1,000 participants, 59 per cent live 'pay check to pay check', 44 per cent have some form of credit-card debt and only 38 per cent have an 'emergency fund' (see section 1.5 below).[32]

These numbers necessitate a response from both private and public sectors. The difficulty lies in accurately measuring and predicting future savings, which in turn makes it harder to legislate, to establish what works and what doesn't. The remainder of this chapter will look at current initiatives in place to promote saving. However, beforehand it is worth briefly considering how individual savings can be measured, how the associated inaccuracy of making predictions can be diminished, and what implications the two theories informing this discussion might have for the UK.

The challenge of accurate measurements and predictions

Milton Friedman's Permanent Income Hypothesis (PIH) remains one of the most influential economic theories attempting to measure permanent income – or the average long-term income over a person's lifetime. PIH was developed in Friedman's *A Theory of the Consumption Function*, first published in 1957.[33] It came largely as a response to Keynesian theory, which struggled to predict long-term rates of savings in relation to changing variables such as income and inflation.

Within PIH, the term 'permanent income' refers to the total long-term average income of an individual or agent. This in turn is determined by the level of assets: physical (property, land etc.); financial (shares, bonds); human (education, experience).

Key within PIH is that a person's propensity to consume is not necessarily driven by current income but rather by future (potential) income – permanent income rather than temporary income plays the larger role in determining consumer spending. Costas Meghir from the Institute of Fiscal Studies points out that Friedman's hypothesis is that:

> individuals base their consumption on a longer-term view of an income measure, perhaps a notion of lifetime wealth or a notion of wealth over a reasonably long horizon. The basic hypothesis posited is that individuals consume a fraction of this permanent income in each period and thus the average propensity to consume would equal the marginal propensity to consume.[34]

This is known as 'consumption smoothing', whereby people would be inclined to smooth out their consumption relative to their permanent income. Consumption smoothing is a departure from the more traditional Keynesian metric of the marginal propensity to consume (MPC). MPC assumes that consumer spending rises – and falls – in line with temporary income, not permanent.

A useful tool for visualising lifetime savings is the Life Cycle of Consumption or the Life Cycle Hypothesis (LCH), first developed in the 1950s by Franco Modigliani and his student Richard Brumberg. Shown in Figure 1.6, LCH makes three broad assumptions:

1. Generally people prefer to smooth out their spending over the long term rather than experience periods of wealth and poverty.
2. People possess varying degrees of impatience in decision-making.
3. People tend to be forward-looking when it comes to spending, assuming future potential income rather than current income.[35]

Just because people would prefer to smooth out their spending over the long term doesn't mean they actually do – quite the contrary.[36] Unpredictability and impatience in relation to volatile levels of income usually lead to volatile levels of consumption or spending. Therefore the consumption line shown in Figure 1.6 is in practice curved, much like the income line. However, LCH uses permanent consumption to illustrate the different periods of savings growth and degrowth across a person's life cycle.

'PIH is inextricably linked to the housing crisis in the UK'

There are issues around the accuracy of economic models in predicting lifetime savings. For instance, Angus Deaton argues that the LCH doesn't fully take into account the issue of uncertainty – something Modigliani himself acknowledged early on.[37] Friedman's PIH has also come under criticism for assuming a constant average propensity to consume. Irwin Friend and Irving B. Kravis argue that within PIH, families with low levels of permanent income are under far more pressure to consume than those with much higher levels.[38]

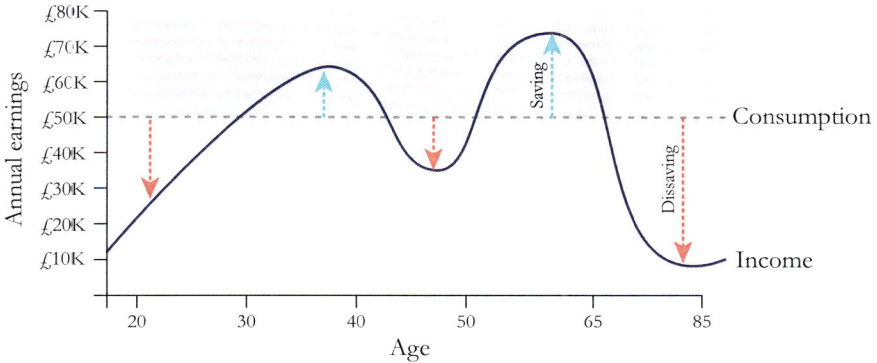

FIGURE 1.6: THE LIFE CYCLE HYPOTHESIS

What do these measurement challenges mean for savings in the UK? The first observation would be that PIH is inextricably linked to the housing crisis in the UK. If the prospect of buying a home is so distant for many households and individuals, it is difficult to encourage saving since financing a purchase is largely dependent on year-on-year income. This in turn raises the question touched on previously about low interest rates. It is unlikely that interest rates will be raised in the short to medium term. Because we live within the open capital markets, ultimately UK rates are determined by world rates. Nevertheless, if people cannot borrow to invest in productive assets – such as homes – because the supply is limited, that will inevitably put downward pressure on interest rates. This comes back to the UK's restrictive planning control on housebuilding. The most productive form of investment for millions has effectively been denied by planning control.

A second observation would be that the welfare state also has a direct impact on PIH. If the government provides for all contingencies and for pensions, what incentives are left to encourage people to save and smooth consumption? Effectively, the state has taken over this role and is doing so through taxation. Therefore the remaining question for low-income households is straightforward: What is the point of saving? Nonetheless, the following section will look at some of the initiatives available for those who, despite this unfavourable environment, remain committed to saving.

1.4   CURRENT INCENTIVES TO PROMOTE SAVING

A few initiatives, public and private, have been implemented to promote saving. However, results seem limited and no single measure stands out as a resounding success. Three main areas need to be addressed:

- Saving for an emergency;
- Saving for a first home;
- Saving for retirement.

Saving for an emergency

Perhaps the most widely used government measure to promote saving has been the tax-free Personal Allowance. For the 2019–20 tax year, every UK citizen and legal worker in the UK is entitled to earn up to £12,500 free of tax.[39] The amount has gradually increased since 1990, when the Personal Allowance stood at just over £3,000.[40]

This comes alongside the Personal Savings Allowance, which for 2019–20 stands at £5,000. However, it only applies for those on lower incomes of up to £17,500 per year. The allowance permits any interest earned on savings to be tax free (again, up to the sum of £5,000). For those earning above £17,500 the allowance is £1,000, falling to £500 for those paying tax at 40 per cent, and for those in the highest tax bracket (45 per cent), it is zero.[41]

Another highly promoted measure has been the Individual Savings Account (ISA), which comes in various formats: Cash ISAs; Stocks and Shares ISAs; Innovative Finance ISAs; Lifetime ISAs. Like the Personal Savings Allowance, ISAs allow individuals to invest up to £20,000 per annum, which grows free from either income tax or capital gains tax. The requirements are to be at least 16 years old for a Cash ISA and 18 for the other forms (the Lifetime ISA is discussed below).[42]

Although very welcome, ISAs remains a difficult and potentionally ineffective tool for directly promoting saving. Indeed, they do not necessarily generate the best returns. In addition, money that is not clearly differentiated risks being spent. ISAs are a halfway house. They are differentiated accounts but there is, for most ISAs, unlimited access to the accumulated capital and interest. Consequently, they function in a different way from, for example, pension savings. Therefore even if a person has surplus net income in a particular tax year, adding that surplus to an ISA does not guarantee any addition to net savings.

'Money that is not clearly differentiated risks being spent'

A more recent and clearly targeted initiative has been the Help to Save scheme. It allows people currently on Working Tax Credit or receiving Universal Credit to get a bonus of 50 pence for every £1 saved over four years. The maximum monthly deposit is £50. This would amount to £2,400 plus £1,200 government bonus over the four-year period, or £3,600[43] – although since the bonus is only paid out in two rounds, at the end of the second and fourth years, the schedule and format of the scheme may not prove attractive to those already on tight budgets. Nonetheless it is a starting point – a Parliamentary report found the scheme: 'a promising approach towards helping lower-income households build precautionary saving. However, at this stage its ambition is limited ... [The Treasury] should give consideration to widening the eligibility criteria in future.'

ISAs are also part of the same government 'package' of initiatives but with the added benefit that they are separate accounts. However, they have experienced inconsistent growth over the past two decades – see Figure 1.7.

Cash ISAs remain by far the most popular option, possibly because they offer great liquidity and minimal risk. The downside is that they also offer minimal reward – particularly in the current low-interest environment. Figure 1.7 shows that there were a total of 10.8 million adult ISA subscriptions in 2017–18, down from 11.1 million in 2016–17.[44]

There are different views as to why the number of ISAs has been declining. Rachel Griffin, a tax planning expert at Quilter, says that low interest rates are making people move their money to higher-risk investments: 'Savers are punishing the low rates on cash offered by banks and building societies, and taking advantage of the opportunity to invest their ISA savings in the stock market.'[45]

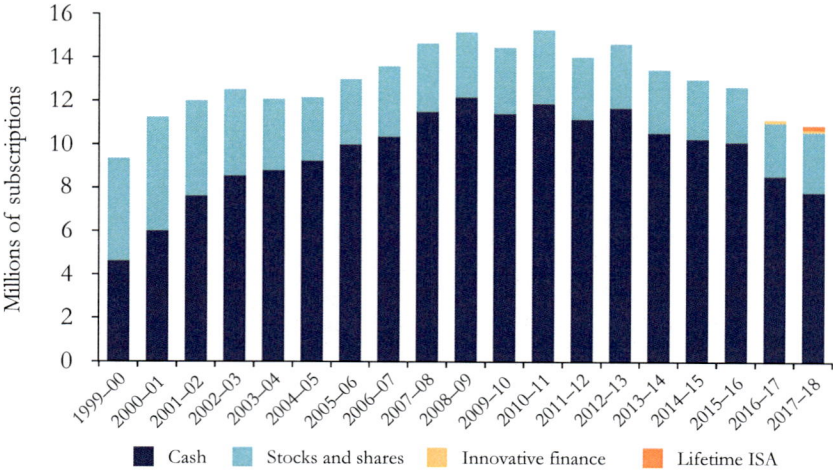

FIGURE 1.7: NUMBER OF ADULT ISA ACCOUNTS SUBSCRIBED TO DURING TAX YEAR

The saving options from the private sector do not appear very attractive either. Most savings accounts offered by the major retail banks come not only with historic low interest rates but also with a list of terms and conditions much of the working population are unable or unwilling to fulfil. Mandatory direct debits, minimum monthly payments, variable interest rates and, in many cases, deposit limits and withdrawal restrictions make high street savings accounts an unappealing option. Andrew Hagger, a personal finance expert at Moneycomms, says:

> The banks have little appetite for customer savings at the moment. The other problem is that mortgage rates have been falling due to competition in the market so if banks lend at lower rates but don't trim savings rates then their margins and profits take a hit.[46]

Saving for a first home

We have already briefly discussed Britain's declining home ownership and seen how the worst hit are young people (25–34-year-olds), of whom some 75 per cent own no form of residential property.[47] Britain's restrictive planning regulations and a growing population have priced homes out of reach for many in society. It is only recently that global economic uncertainty and Brexit have mildly brought prices down, particularly in London and the affluent south-east, which were already in a housing bubble.[48]

The Lifetime ISA (LISA) and Help To Buy are two of the most commonly used saving schemes available to first-time buyers. The LISA can either be used for retirement or purchasing a first property. LISA account holders can deposit up to £4,000 per year and receive a 25 per cent government bonus on top, or £1,000. After five years a person who has deposited £4,000 per year will have £20,000 plus the government bonus of £5,000, totalling £25,000. Alternatively they can continue contributing to this account and use the total sum for retirement after the age of 65. If someone makes the maximum annual contribution of £4,000 from the age of 18 to 65, they will have received £33,000 in government bonuses for their retirement.[49]

Unlike LISAs, the Help to Buy scheme may only be used for purchasing a first property. The maximum property price covered is £600,000 in England and £300,000 in Wales. Help to Buy works as a type of government equity loan: a buyer puts down a 5 per cent deposit for a mortgage, to which the government will add a 20 per cent loan, effectively making the total deposit 25 per cent (within London the 20 per cent rises to 40 per cent).[50]

Help to Buy received mixed reviews. While it can help those without much disposable income on to the housing ladder, in some areas it has pushed up prices – to the benefit merely of estate agents and developers.[51] A Parliamentary report found that while the scheme has encouraged the construction of new homes, only 37 per cent of all recipients needed the financial assistance, implying over 60 per cent could have managed without.[52] Another problem arises from the government's right to change interest rates after five years. According to Meg Hillier MP, Chair of the House of Commons Public Accounts Committee: 'The scheme exposes both the government and consumers to significant financial risks were house prices or interest rates to change ... It does not help make homes more affordable nor address other pressing housing problems in the sector.'

Saving for retirement

Unlike saving for an emergency or for property, saving for retirement benefits from a more robust legislative framework – not least because of the associated long history and wealth of administrative experience. The 'Old Age' state pension was first introduced in Britain in 1908 to around 500,000 people over the age of 70. All in that category were entitled to a monthly payment (£21 at the time), though only one in four of the population would live to the qualifying age.[53]

The 'triple lock' system introduced by the coalition government in 2010 ensures that each year the basic state pension will rise by the rate of inflation, average earnings growth or a minimum of 2.5 per cent – whichever is largest.[54]

A number of concerns have been expressed regarding the long-term feasibility of the triple-lock guarantee. A report by the Institute for Fiscal Studies (IFS) has found that:

> Between April 2010 and April 2016 the value of the state pension has been increased by 22.2 per cent, compared to growth in earnings of 7.6 per cent and growth in prices of 12.3 per cent over the same period.[55]

This means that pension growth was triple the earnings growth over the same period. Frank Field MP, Chair of the House of Commons Work and Pensions Committee, has said that keeping the triple lock could cost the taxpayer an additional £50 billion over the period up to 2050 and shift retirement age from 65 to 70.[56]

Private pensions or workplace pensions have been an area of significant growth. The government's Automatic Enrolment initiative means that all employees over the age of 22 and earning above £10,000 per year are enrolled in a workplace scheme. However, employees may opt out if they explicitly request to do so.

Research conducted by the IFS reveals strong growth rates in private workplace pensions, doubling from 32 per cent of all employees in 2012 to 67 per cent in 2018.[57] The increase in workplace contributions is likely to have a positive impact on retirement savings in the long run. However, sustainability issues remain for those who are ineligible and out of work, unable to work, self-employed or who earn less than £10,000 per year.

1.5   SAVINGS IN THE USA

It is useful to consider some of the measures used in the USA to promote saving. Figure 1.8 shows the Personal Savings Rate, which represents the ratio of personal income saved to personal net income over time. As shown, rates of saving peaked in the 1970s but then dropped steadily, reaching a historic low of just 2.2 per cent in 2005.

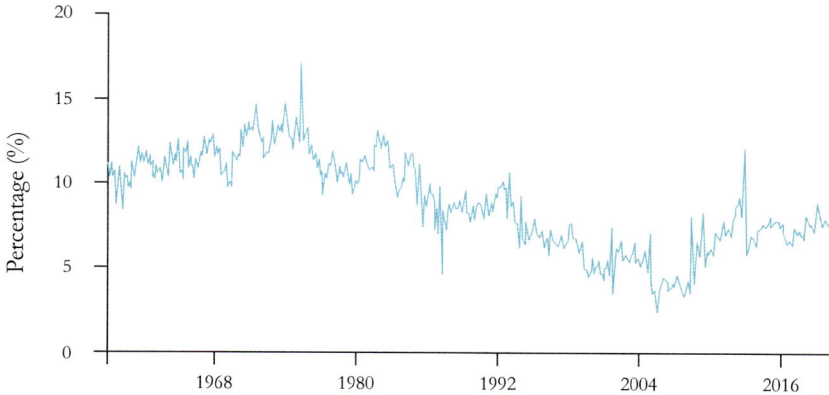

FIGURE 1.8: USA PERSONAL SAVINGS RATE, 1959–2020

Whereas Americans had tended to spend below their income, as the economy performed well, particularly since the 1970s/80s, they began to spend more relative to saving, many exceeding their net disposable income: as of March 2020, the average credit-card debt is estimated to be $5,700, and 41.2 per cent of all households carry some form of it.[58]

The Personal Savings Rate gradually recovered since the 2005 low, and as of January 2020 stands at around 7.9 per cent. The risks associated with a lack of savings in the long run outweigh any short-term benefits to the economy. A report by the Global Markets Institute on the importance of long-term savings argues that they 'are like ladders that are used to bring opportunity and security within greater reach'.[59]

However, the ability to save varies greatly depending on the income bracket. Figure 1.9 shows that around 80 per cent of US earners in the top 10 per cent are able to save as opposed to just 30 per cent in the bottom 20 per cent.[60] This probably comes as no surprise since low income is the most important deterrent to the long-term accumulation of savings. A report by Deloitte found that: 'Inability to save not only impedes some semblance of financial security – to handle unfavourable events such as a job loss or sudden illness – but also dents asset accumulation, a reason why wealth inequality has gone up in recent years.'[61]

'The ability to save varies greatly'

A lack of asset accumulation for those at the lower end of the income ladder is the key issue. However, it must also be recalled that the USA has succeeded in increasing the Personal Savings Rate from the all-time low of 2005 (albeit with some volatility during the peak of the financial crisis of 2007–8). This was due in part to a post-recession change in attitude to spending but also to a variety of initiatives that encourage saving for US citizens.

The '401k' and the Individual Retirement Accounts (IRAs) remain perhaps the best known of these initiatives. The 401k is a defined-contribution plan whereby the employer and the employee pay into the account. Usually the funds are invested in stocks and shares for an extended period. Being a 'qualified plan' it is eligible for certain tax benefits. The advantage of the 401k is that it is a great vehicle for accumulating retirement savings by reaping the benefits of long-term compounded interest within a tax-efficient framework.

By comparison, only since 2018 has the UK's Pensions Regulator made it compulsory for all employers to offer 'automatic enrolment' into a workplace pension scheme. The 401k in the USA dates back to 1978, and as of 2016 there were over 55 million active accounts, with an estimated $5.9 trillion in assets.[62] There may also be cultural/attitudinal differences here: the responsibility to provide is more entrenched in the USA than in the UK.

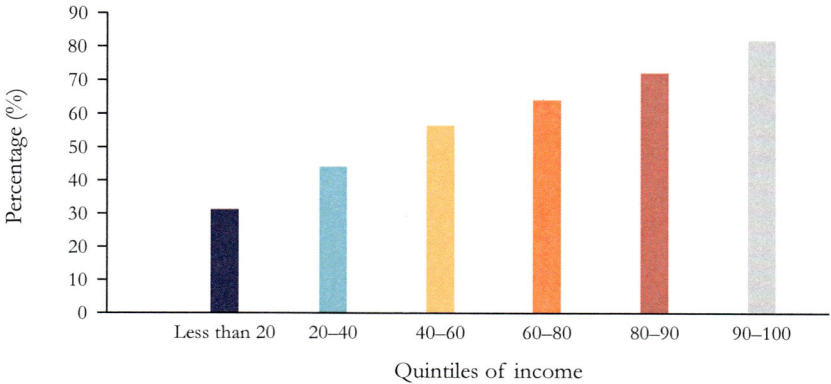

FIGURE 1.9: SHARE OF US HOUSEHOLDS THAT SAVE GOES UP WITH INCOME

The USA has also introduced newer initiatives, such as the Individual Development Accounts (IDAs) aimed at low-income asset building or home ownership. IDAs are effectively contribution-matching savings plans that enable the beneficiary to save towards the purchase of real estate, post-secondary education or a business. The vision behind them is that they 'introduce real assets into the lives of many poor people who would otherwise be without them ... IDAs enable the poor to bring their own cards to the table and make their own deal.'[63] Further US initiatives include Children's Savings Accounts and Saver's Credit.

There are lessons to be learnt from the USA's growth in savings since 2005. This is not to say that government-led initiatives are necessarily the only answer, but government and civil society must play a role in turning the tide and producing a change in attitudes towards saving. Only a robust message on the importance of saving, coupled with clear policy on the avenues to save, can bring the outcomes many desire.

NOTES TO CHAPTER 1

1   Dato Kim Tan, 'Covid Lessons: We are Not all in the Same Boat', *Christian Responsibility in Public Affairs*, May 2020.

2   Kate Hughes, 'Coronavirus turns UK into a Nation of Savers', *The Independent*, 12 May 2020; https://www.independent.co.uk/money/spend-save/coronavirus-saving-emergency-furloughed-income-redundant-recession-bills-a9509816.html.

3   Harry Brennan, 'Coronavirus has turned Britain into a Nation of Savers Squirrelling away £162 a week', 11 May 2020; https://www.telegraph.co.uk/personal-banking/savings/coronavirus-has-turned-britain-nation-savers-squirreling-away.

4   Hughes, 'Coronavirus turns UK into a nation of savers'.

5   'Coronavirus: Poorer Households funding Lockdown with Debt, says Think Tank', *BBC News*, 22 June 2020; https://www.bbc.co.uk/news/business-53131643.

6   Ibid.

7   Daniel Clark, 'Gross Domestic Product (GDP) Year-on-Year Growth in the United Kingdom (UK) from 1949 to 2019', Statista, February 2020; https://www.statista.com/statistics/281734/gdp-growth-in-the-united-kingdom-uk.

8   Charlie Barton, 'Saving Statistics', Finder.com, 20 August 2019; https://www.finder.com/uk/saving-statistics.

9   Ibid.

10 Nathan Mladin and Barbara Ridpath, *Forgive Us Our Debts: Lending and Borrowing as if Relationships Matter*, London: Theos, 2019, p. 34.

11 Ibid.

12 Office for National Statistics, 'Average Household Income, UK: Financial Year ending 2019 (Provisional)'; https://www.ons.gov.uk/peoplepopulationandcommunity/personalandhouseholdfinances/incomeandwealth/bulletins/householddisposableincomeandinequality/financialyearending2019provisional.

13 House of Commons Treasury Committee, 'Household Finances: Income, Saving and Debt; Nineteenth Report of Session 2017–19', p. 4.

14 UK Parliament, 'Publications and Records', 26 July 2018; https://publications.parliament.uk/pa/cm201719/cmselect/cmtreasy/565/56504.htm.

15 Office for National Statistics, 'International Comparisons of UK Productivity (ICP), Final Estimates: 2016', 6 April 2018, pp. 2–4.

16 Chris Giles, 'Britain's Productivity Crisis in Eight Charts – Slowdown in Output Per Hour Worked has Many Facets', *Financial Times*, 13 August 2018; https://www.ft.com/content/6ada0002-9a57-11e8-9702-5946bae86e6d.

17 Treasury Committee, 'Household Finances', p. 5.

18 Ibid., p. 6.

19 Ibid., p. 7.

20 Google – Public Data from World Bank, 'UK Life Expectancy', October 2019; https://www.google.com/publicdata/explore?ds=d5bncppjof8f9_&ctype=l&s trail=false&bcs=d&nselm=h&met_y=sp_dyn_le00_in&scale_y=lin&ind_y=f alse&rdim=region&idim=country:GBR&ifdim=region&hl=en&dl=en&ind= false.

21 Migration Watch, 'Net Migration Statistics', November 2019; https://www.migrationwatchuk.org/statistics-net-migration-statistics.

22 Google – Public Data from World Bank, 'Birth Rates UK', October 2019; https://www.google.com/publicdata/explore?ds=d5bncppjof8f9_&ctype=l& strail=false&bcs=d&nselm=h&met_y=sp_dyn_tfrt_in&scale_y=lin&ind_y= false&rdim=region&idim=country:GBR:USA:JPN&ifdim=region&tstart=- 291081600000&tend=1476140400000&hl=en&dl=en&ind=false.

23 Office for National Statistics, 'Overview of UK Population', July 2017, p. 11.

24 Ibid.

25 Government Office for Science, 'Future of an Ageing Population', 2016; https://www.gov.uk/government/publications/future-of-an-ageing-population.

26 Bank of England, 'Interest Rates and Bank Rate', November 2019; https://www.bankofengland.co.uk/monetary-policy/the-interest-rate-bank-rate.

27 Martin Lewis, 'Regular Savings Accounts', Money Saving Expert; https://www.moneysavingexpert.com/savings/best-regular-savings-accounts.

28 Treasury Committee, 'Household Finances', p. 6.

29 Barton, 'Saving Statistics'.

30 Ibid.

31 Brian Milligan, 'Millions have less than £100 in Savings, Study finds', *BBC News*, 29 September 2016; https://www.bbc.co.uk/news/business-37504449.

32 2019 Schwab Modern Wealth Survey; https://www.aboutschwab.com/modernwealth2019.

33 Milton Friedman, *A Theory of the Consumption Function*, Princeton, NJ: Princeton University Press, 1957.

34 Costas Meghir, 'A Retrospective on Friedman's Theory of Permanent Income', Institute for Fiscal Studies, January 2004, p. 3.

35 Flora Mae Z. Agustin, Patrisha Marie A. Ambrosio, Emerita Mhiro H. Mones and Eleanor P. Garoy, 'Intertemporal Life-Cycle Theory of Consumption', 13th National Convention on Statistics, October 2016, Mandaluyong City, Philippines.

36 Martin Browning and Thomas F. Crossley, 'The Lifecycle Model of Consumption and Saving', *Journal of Economic Perspectives* 15:3, Summer 2001, pp. 3–22.

37 Angus Deaton, 'Franco Modigliani and the Life Cycle Theory of Consumption', *BNL Quarterly Review* 58:233–4, 2005, pp. 91–107.

38 Deepali Pal, 'Permanent Income Hypothesis: Subject-Matter, Reconciliation and Criticisms | Consumption Function', *Economics Discussion*, November 2019; http://www.economicsdiscussion.net/consumption-function/permanent-income-hypothesis-subject-matter-reconciliation-and-criticisms-consumption-function/14473.

39 Her Majesty's Revenue & Customs (HMRC), 'Official Statistics, Income Tax Personal Allowances and Reliefs', July 2019.

40 Ibid.

41 Money Advice Service, 'Tax on Savings and Investments – how it works', September 2019; https://www.moneyadviceservice.org.uk/en/articles/your-tax-rate.

42 GOV.UK, 'Individual Savings Accounts (ISAs)', July 2019; https://www.gov.uk/individual-savings-accounts.

43 GOV.UK – 'Help to Save', July 2019; https://www.gov.uk/get-help-savings-low-income/what-youll-get.

44 Tom Bailey, 'Latest Isa statistics: Cash Isa sales slump as Savers turn to the Stockmarket', *Money Observer*, 1 May 2019; https://www.moneyobserver.com/news/latest-isa-statistics-cash-isa-sales-slump-savers-turn-to-stockmarket.

45 Ibid.

46 Grace Gausden, 'Banks cull one of the last decent Options available to Savers: HSBC and First Direct slash Interest on Regular Savings Accounts from 5 per cent to 2.75 per cent', *This is Money*, 17 October 2019; https://www.thisismoney.co.uk/money/saving/article-7583359/HSBC-Direct-slash-regular-savings-account-rates.html.

47 Treasury Committee, 'Household Finances', p. 6.

48 Joe Curtis, 'London House Prices suffer Steepest Fall since Financial Crisis', *City A.M.*, 10 October 2019; https://www.cityam.com/london-house-prices-suffer-steepest-fall-since-financial-crisis.

49 Martin Lewis, 'Lifetime ISAs', Money Saving Expert; https://www.moneysavingexpert.com/savings/lifetime-isas.

50 GOV.UK, 'Affordable Home Ownership Schemes: Help to Buy', September 2019 https://www.gov.uk/affordable-home-ownership-schemes/help-to-buy-equity-loan.

51 Kate Hughes, 'Help to Buy Scheme pushed up House Prices, Study Finds', *The Independent*, 14 June 2019; https://www.independent.co.uk/money/spend-save/help-to-buy-house-prices-loans-first-time-buyers-savings-a8958056.html.

52 House of Commons – Committee of Public Accounts, 'Help to Buy: Equity Loan Scheme; One Hundred and Fourteenth Report of Session 2017–19'; https://www.parliament.uk/business/committees/committees-a-z/commons-select/public-accounts-committee/news-parliament-2017/help-to-buy-report-published-17-19.

53 State Pension Age, 'History of State Pension Age', November 2019; http://www.web40571.clarahost.co.uk/statepensionage/SPA_history.htm.

54 Phillip Inman, 'Pensions Triple Lock: What you Need to Know', *The Guardian*, 27 April 2017; https://www.theguardian.com/money/2017/apr/27/pensions-triple-lock-questions-answered.

55 Carl Emmerson, 'Would you Rather? Further Increases in the State Pension age v Abandoning the Triple Lock', Institute for Fiscal Studies, 27 Feb 2017; https://www.ifs.org.uk/publications/8942.

56 'Frank Field calls for Scrapping of "Triple Lock". People would Need to Retire in their 70s', *Professional Adviser*, 28 February 2017; https://www.professionaladviser.com/professional-adviser/news/3005488/frank-field-calls-for-scrapping-of-triple-lock.

57 Rowena Crawford, Jonathan Cribb and Carl Emmerson, 'More into Workplace Pensions: Minimum Default Pension Contributions rise for most Employees and their Employers', Institute for Fiscal Studies, 5 April 2018; https://www.ifs.org.uk/publications/12895.

58 Joe Resendiz, 'Average Credit Card Debt in America: July 2020', *Value Penguin*, 17 June 2020; https://www.valuepenguin.com/average-credit-card-debt.

59 Suzanne Nora Johnson, Lisa Mensah and C. Eugene Steuerle, 'Savings in America: Building Opportunities for All', Global Markets Institute at Goldman Sachs, Spring 2006; http://dx.doi.org/10.2139/ssrn.981644, p. 3.

60 Akrur Barua, 'Personal Savings: A Look at how Americans are saving', Deloitte, August 2019; https://www2.deloitte.com/us/en/insights/economy/spotlight/economics-insights-analysis-08-2019.html.

61 Ibid.

62 Investment Company Institute, 'Frequently Asked Questions About 401(k) Plan Research'; https://www.ici.org/faqs/faq/401k/faqs_401k.

63 Office of Policy Development and Research (PD&R), 'Individual Development Accounts: A Vehicle for Low-Income Asset Building and Homeownership', Fall 2012; https://www.huduser.gov/portal/periodicals/em/fall12/highlight2.html.

CHAPTER 2

THE PRINCIPLES OF MONEY AND SAVINGS

2.1   A BRIEF HISTORY

Where does the iconic piggy bank come from, and why is the name associated with a farm animal? Its origins are not just derived from the visual resemblance but from the material itself. Throughout the Middle Ages, households in England would save their coins in kitchenware made from a clay known as 'pygg'. In time the visual and linguistic resemblance evolved into the modern-day piggy bank.

However, piggy banks from fifteenth-century England had a very important distinction: there was no underside plug or hole. Once the coin went in, there was no going back. In order to retrieve the money the piggy bank would have to be smashed – hence the expression 'breaking the bank'. According to Professor Colin Mayer:

> the fact that the piggy bank had to be destroyed to retrieve its money made its destruction a very deliberate decision ... Savings were a considered commitment to put aside money for a particular purpose or for a rainy day when it was needed – unlike the piggy banks of today.[1]

Savings carried far greater weight, literally and figuratively, and families and individuals had a more profound understanding and awareness of the value of saving. So why has the aspiration to build savings seemingly dwindled in popularity? To answer this we need to go back to the very origins of money and wealth.

Money is effectively stored value. A country's national currency is a standardised measure of value that can be exchanged for goods and services. *Lexico* defines 'money' as: 'A current medium of exchange in the form of coins and banknotes'.[2] In lay terms it represents an easy and effective way of exchanging goods and services, and prior to 'money' in this sense, commodities and goods served as currency.

Such diverse commodities as cocoa, wheat, cattle and cigarettes all have in common that they have been exchanged as a form of currency. Almonds were popular in parts of India, corn in Guatemala, rice in most of South East Asia – and the Norwegians used butter as currency throughout the mediaeval era.[3] The very term 'salary' comes from the Latin *sal*, meaning 'salt'. Throughout the Roman world many were paid in salt – a highly valued commodity,[4] particularly given the bland food most were used to.

Despite the increasingly widespread use of banknotes and coins, valuable commodities continued to act as currency in different parts of the world where institutionalised prohibitions were in place. Under the former Soviet Union, western beverages such as Pepsi, Marlboro cigarettes, foreign items of clothing such as American jeans and branded t-shirts regularly passed through several hands before being consumed or used (if used at all). The vacuum created by restrictions was quickly filled by valuable goods. In many countries, even today, gold, jewellery and artworks remain commonly used forms of currency and of storing value.

What does all this say about money itself? We may say that it has two dimensions: the purely functional and the wider cultural and societal. If goods represent value, then money – in the form of notes and coins – is a more efficient and effective way of storing value. It is far safer to store your wealth in copper coins than in spices or cocoa beans. This may seem obvious but the initial arrival of the monetary system revolutionised societies. It enabled the open marketplace and powered the rapid exchange of goods and services, which in turn led to unparalleled cultural and economic transformation.

Savings and human nature in classical thought

First, it is important to distinguish between savings and wealth. While wealth can be understood as a form of accumulated savings, for our purposes savings represent a form of financial security in providing

41

'It is important to distinguish between savings and wealth'

for basic needs such as food and shelter. Wealth, on the other hand, can represent a form of savings that goes beyond these needs, a surplus available for leisure activities or luxury goods. We need to consider both for a better understanding of savings, broadening the discussion by looking at historical attitudes towards the use and function of money.

The advent of the Greek civilisation represents the most conspicuous outcome of the first monetary system and its positive impact on development. The monetisation of value created – and elevated – a new society: one centred around trade and the marketplace. Herodotus recorded how the ancient kingdom of Lydia was the first to use coinage and establish trading shops as early as the seventh and sixth centuries BC.[5] Coins provided an unprecedented level of stability in the marketplace. They became the benchmark against which all other commodities and services were valued. And unlike salt or wheat, coins were highly portable and resistant to degradation.

The results for people and society were dramatic. According to Professor Jack Weatherford:

> The greatness of Greece came as a by-product of the monetary and mercantile revolution from Lydia, the introduction of money, modern markets, and wholesale and retail distribution. Money made possible the organization of society on a scale much greater and far more complex than either kinship or force could have achieved.
>
> ... virtually everything could be expressed in terms of a common denominator – money ... from a loaf of bread to a poem, from an hour's sexual services to taxes, or from a rack of lamb to a month's rent.[6]

This brings us back to the first observation about money: its pure functionality turns out to be a formidable force in enabling and facilitating the market-based economy. The investor Ray Dalio compares the economy to a machine comprised of the total sum of transactions; that is, all buyers and sellers.[7] Akin to the intricate parts of a mechanical watch movement, the economy also functions in different cycles and sectors that turn each other at varying speeds. It is critical, therefore, that all the parts keep moving. Should one fail, the entire mechanism risks coming to a halt. Money is the lubricant that enables the economic machine to run smoothly.

Yet money often goes far beyond its mere functional role as an enabler or facilitator: it has impacts on the spiritual as well the material; it alters and shapes behaviour; it changes tradition; it builds and destroys relationships. Money transcends the economic and enters the cultural and social spheres of society. Nowhere is this more evident than in the early writings of the ancient Greek and Roman philosophers, who wrestled with its role and use.

It would be useful to define the terminology. What do we mean by 'wealth' at a societal level? Again, at its most functional level, wealth, as Adam Smith wrote in *The Wealth of Nations*, is society's 'annual produce of the land and labour', produce here referring to items or skills that have economic value and can therefore be used in transactions.[8] Wealth in this case can be understood as valuable financial assets generated from an inheritance, an act of goodwill or from profit. Smith was distinctive in his understanding of wealth as the total production of a country rather than its net assets (which would become GDP in modern times), while the United Nations goes beyond the material and defines 'inclusive wealth' as both economic growth and the well-being of the people.[9] We will return to Smith and his understanding of human behaviour in relation to money shortly.

There is no clear agreement among the ancient philosophers on how money ought to be used – and not abused. However, there is an almost unanimous rejection of accumulating wealth driven by greed and a materialistic infatuation with the self. The irony, of course, is that most of the ancient philosophers were from the wealthier upper classes – education and social status went hand in hand.

In Plato's *Republic* the need for the state originates from a collective necessity to congregate with others in order to have the needs of society met. Again, not everyone is fit to rule in this society, rather only the two upper classes: the rulers and the 'guardians'[10] – and not out of any particular desire or privilege to rule but rather to avoid being ruled by the lower classes. Plato identifies three rewards that life in the Republic has to offer: profit, wisdom and victory. Of the three, profit is the least valuable.[11]

Plato is aware of the necessity of material goods but also concerned that the pursuit of wealth corrupts both the individual and society. In the second book of the *Republic* he records the dialogue between Socrates and Glaucon:

> I see; you want not only a State, but a luxurious State; and possibly in the more complex frame we may sooner find justice and injustice. Then the fine arts must go to work – every conceivable instrument and ornament of luxury will be wanted. There will be dancers, painters, sculptors, musicians, cooks, barbers, tire-women [i.e. ladies' maids], nurses, artists; swineherds and neatherds too for the animals, and physicians to cure the disorders of which luxury is the source ... And so, as time goes on, and they advance in the pursuit of wealth, the more they hold that in honour the less they honour virtue. May not the opposition of wealth and virtue be conceived as if each lay in the scale of a balance inclining opposite ways?[12]

The dichotomy between wealth and virtue leads to an outright battle – one comes at the expense of the other. It is clearly favourable for the just man to concentrate his efforts on attaining virtue rather than wealth. In Plato's dialogues the power of wealth in creating a 'luxurious State' has profoundly corrupting effects on the character of its citizens. Even something as essential as loaning money is to be strictly forbidden – the risks of overspending are too high and the reputational consequences of failing to repay too great. However, Plato did agree to amical, interest-free loans not bound by any contractual agreement.[13] He overlooked the potential for financial development and focused almost exclusively on the negative social implications. His satirical rhetoric, above, that we will 'need physicians to cure the disorders of which luxury is the source' cements his understanding of wealth as a corrupting indulgence.[14]

The Stoics fared no better – their generally bleak outlook on life's occurrences meant that wealth and material possessions were viewed as a source of anxiety and sorrow. They thought that while external occurrences lie beyond our control, our reaction to them does not. Thus Seneca the Younger wrote:

> He who craves riches feels fear on their account. No man, however, enjoys a blessing that brings anxiety; he is always trying to add a little more. While he puzzles over increasing his wealth, he forgets how to use it.[15]

Again, like many of his contemporaries Seneca critiqued wealth from a position of wealth. In some sense, poverty for him almost had a noble characteristic. Yet as historians of Stoicism point out, it was not intended as 'something to be sought after'.[16]

Nonetheless, the Roman world promoted private property and, much like the Greek, fully witnessed the monetisation of goods and services and the impact it had on Roman society. However, Roman philosophers seldom fantasised about wealth as something belonging to the community rather than the individual (as in Plato's *Republic* for example). The fact that wealth can be managed and taxed became one of the main pillars that upheld Roman society and Rome's expansion into an imperial power.

The culture of consumerism

The Greek and Roman philosophers spoke about money mainly in terms of wealth and excess. Yet here we are trying to develop a vision that fosters the healthy and prudent use of money within a culture increasingly prone to spend rather than save. It is important to note the link between money, consumerism and a lack of savings. While money, savings and the associated problems existed long before consumerism in the modern sense, a culture of excessive consumerism threatens the ethos of saving: it erodes savings and can lead to impoverishment rather than financial stability. In other words, it can be in opposition to saving at the level of a particular individual or household, even though the free market has increased overall prosperity to society as a whole.

There is little debating that proliferation of the enterprise economy over the last century has generated unprecedented levels of human development and global wealth. The standard of living has been raised for billions around the world. Innovative competition has brought products and services to those for whom until recently they would have been out of reach. There are fewer people around the world living on less than $1.90 per day than at any time in recorded history. Over 1 billion people have been lifted out of poverty in the last 25 years and it is expected that extreme poverty will be eradicated by 2030.[17] The merits of free enterprise are well documented, but we are faced with remaining questions around the responsible use of money and the ability to save within a post-recession environment that still fails to reward saving.

'Consumerism was the "-ism" that won' the twentieth century, writes Gary Cross in his seminal book *An All-Consuming Century*.[18] No single political belief or ideology succeeded – rather consumerism did, because it enabled people to express the cardinal ideals of the century: liberty and democracy. Consumption freed individuals to express themselves in this newly dynamic, mass-production society.[19] It redefined western democracy, transcended politics and transformed culture.

One definition of consumerism points to the inclination that 'the free choice of consumers should strongly orient the choice [of] what is produced and how, and therefore [result in] the economic organization of a society.'[20] An abstract view of consumerism points to a socio-economic phenomenon that collectively shapes – and creates – the marketplace. It has two prominent dimensions: economic and cultural.

Economic consumerism

Economic consumerism only became part of public discourse following the industrial revolution and the subsequent arrival of mass production. Thus it was from around the beginning of the twentieth century that a growing middle class could buy machine-manufactured goods en masse. Consumerism became the new economic dictum of industry and the marketplace. It created a society in which the consumer is effectively the deciding factor in what products and companies succeed or fail – determining where capital is allocated. John Bugas, a senior Ford Motor Company executive, said in 1955: 'The term "consumerism" would pin the tag where [power] actually belongs – on Mr. Consumer, the real boss and beneficiary of the American system.'[21]

From an economic point of view, consumerism brings benefits. It offers choice, promotes competition and, in the medium to long term, protects the consumer by enabling good products to succeed and bad to fail. It also encourages market diversity and technological development. The variety of demand brought by consumerism ensures that each price-point is fulfilled – from the cheapest to the most expensive.

'People could afford to buy things out of want, not need'

Of course, the same favourable outcomes can be credited to the free market more broadly, but it was only after the industrial revolution of the eighteenth and nineteenth centuries that GDP per capita experienced a meteoric rise. Research conducted by the Bank of England has yielded the startling revelation that between about 1000 BC and the 1750s, economic growth averaged 0.1 per cent per year;[22] that is, living standards were essentially flat for 3,000 years. However, GDP per capita in industrialised countries such as the USA, Japan and the UK rose from of $750 in 1800 to $2,500 in 1900. Even on a global scale, a report by the OECD found that:

> since the 1820s the average GDP per capita of the world's population has increased by a factor of 10, a growth that contributed immensely to increased economic well-being. No region or country saw its real income decline over this long period.[23]

In her book *Bourgeois Equality*, Deirdre McCloskey gives some even more startling statistics. She suggests that growth per capita across the world has been between 30- and 100-fold over the last two centuries.[24]

This had a tremendous effect on people and society: for the first time a significant section of the population could afford products that go beyond the strict necessities (i.e. food and shelter). People could afford to buy things out of want, not need. Bernard Mandeville was probably the first major figure to comprehend the magnitude of this transformation and consider its wider implications. In his most popular work, *The Fable of the Bees*, first published in 1714, he went against the puritan influences sweeping England and argued in favour of luxury or 'vanity' spending as a means to a more prosperous and healthy society for all – one in which the needs of the poor and the disenfranchised could be met through the economic growth generated by increased spending, though more state-directed than Adam Smith's laissez-faire. The closing lines of his poem read:

> Bare Virtue can't make Nations live
> In Splendor; they, that would revive
> A Golden Age, must be as free,
> For Acorns, as for Honesty.[25]

This brought Mandeville into some conflict with prevailing Christian beliefs about virtue. Nevertheless, for all its ills and woes, mass production marked a historically unprecedented rise in standards of living – a transformation often overlooked in today's public discourse.

Cultural consumerism

It is in relation to cultural consumerism that the most contentious issues lie. In some sense the economic dimension considers the 'how' and the cultural dimension the 'why' – much like the Greek and Roman philosophers discussed above.

Perhaps the most glaring critique of consumerism is that it can take over and go beyond the financial transactions themselves. Attachment to objects can act as a substitute for human relationships (e.g. smartphones). Human vulnerability may also lead to an unhealthy relationship between one's spending and physical and mental well-being.

Biologically speaking, the reason is simple: buying gives a mood lift, providing a quick release of the body's natural pleasure endorphins, dopamine and serotonin. The problem is that the pleasure is often short lived and the 'crash' usually leaves the buyer feeling guilty. Dr Brad Klontz has written extensively on the issue of compulsive spending and found that: 'Emotionally charged circumstances make us prone to overspending. If we're rationally challenged, we're financially challenged.'[26] This would explain, at least in part, why so many have a preponderance to overspend and place themselves in challenging financial situations. Research also suggests that people are most prone to overspend in two extremes: when they're feeling either down (e.g. a relationship breakdown or traumatic life event) or up (e.g. going away on holiday, a new promotion, a new house).[27] There are clear triggers that promote overspending – be they positive or negative.

This is of quite some relevance to cultural consumerism. Consumerism cannot be understood in silos. It has to be recognised as a complex web of economic, social and even biological factors that collectively make up the macro concept.

Therefore cultural consumerism is mostly viewed negatively, seen as a feeble form of short-term gratification. In popular culture this can be summed up by a take on 'keeping up with the Joneses' once

'Genuine acts of generosity and benevolence should not be ignored'

attributed to, among others, the actor Walter Slezak: 'Spending money you don't have for things you don't need, to impress people you don't like.'[28] Consumerism and social interactions are deeply intertwined. Possessions can become a benchmark for status, self-gratification or the desire to give skewed appearances. They can become a game of compare and contrast: Does my neighbour have more than I do? How can I get more than my neighbour?

Yet genuine acts of generosity and benevolence should not be ignored. As we have seen, spending and mass production have enabled greater generosity by drastically raising the standards of living for everyone. However, even something like giving gifts can have a negative connotation if done with the wrong intentions.

During his Christmas speech of 2012, Pope Benedict XVI said that 'Within a society of consumerism, we are tempted to seek joy in things ... Christmas is not an external celebration ... but one that honours the Son of God.'[29] Similarly, Pope Francis wrote in a Homily that consumerism goes against the very spirit of generosity: 'excessive spending to buy more than we need – is a lack of austerity in life. This is the enemy of generosity.'[30]

Of course, another critique is the environmental impact: unlimited consumption cannot be sustained with limited resources. Unless sustainable solutions are found, the needs of a global population of more than 7 billion will continue to place increased demand on limited resources. The 2019 UN Global Resources Outlook report found that the 'majority of growth in resource extraction has occurred in upper-middle income countries, who increased their global share of domestic material consumption from 33 per cent in 1970 to 56 per cent in 2017'.[31] Growth and increased demand in the emerging markets have contributed to a tripling of natural-resource extractions over the last 40 years.

The moral dilemma

We need to find the right moral balance between promoting economic growth and lifting people out of poverty, and encouraging a form of 'responsible consumerism' in which people can – and should – enjoy the fruits of their labour but with an increased awareness about consumerism and financial stability.

Thus irresponsible spending can only be countered effectively through a greater understanding of money and budgeting. Wealth can be a blessing and a curse – as the saying goes: 'Money is a good servant but a terrible master'.

Indeed, the ancient philosophers were attacking excessive indulgence in wealth, while modern consumerism is more of a shadow or imitation of this. However, the main difference is that consumerism can lead to poverty or precarious financial situations for those who lack prudence in financial affairs. This raises questions around the role and use of money.

Another socio-economic issue is increasing complexity. The social and material are no longer clearly defined, modern shopping centres being a good example of this, having become as much about social activities (e.g. dining, cinema) as shopping, as well as increasingly serving as venues for community events such as theatre and live music.

Jon Goss wrote an intriguing article entitled 'The Magic of the Mall'. He analysed in depth the plethora of psychological, physical and emotional strategies aimed at the consumer with the sole aim of promoting spending: 'Developers and designers of the retail-built environment exploit the power of place and an intuitive understanding of the structuration of space to facilitate consumption ... They strive to present an alternative rationale for the shopping centre's existence.'[32]

On some level it is hard not to conclude that consumers have been preyed upon. They are under the influence of so many concealed forces that at times it feels rather immoral. Could spending in such an environment be managed responsibly? Moreover, would a cultural change promote a change in spending habits? This is the remaining challenge.

2.2   PRUDENCE AS VIRTUE

Adam Smith – as much ethicist and social philosopher as economist – wrote extensively about the virtuous person and the 'good society'. Indeed, *The Theory of Moral Sentiments* lays out the blueprint for the desirable human behavioural characteristics that might lead to an upright and noble society. Key in Smith's argument is that we can better understand human moral action through psychology and a study of the social sciences than through pure reason.[33]

'Moral action is not solely a calculated act' Smith was above all a fervid social observer. In *The Theory of Moral Sentiments* he exposes how moral human action lies between two often contrasting traits: self-interest and sympathy.[34] When faced with the suffering or joy of others, a part of us instinctively shares in the negative or positive emotions even though the causal event has no direct impact on us. Smith argues that no matter how self-absorbed we may be, as social beings we display a degree of empathy or sympathy towards others:

> How selfish soever man may be supposed, there are evidently some principles in his nature, which interest him in the fortune of others, and render their happiness necessary to him, though he derives nothing from it, except the pleasure of seeing it.[35]

Yet this empathising is of course limited. We share in the mourning of a mother who has lost her child but we do not mourn as she does. We are happy for a friend who has passed an exam but not as happy as they are. Of course, there are exceptions to the rule but as a basis for explaining human morality, Smith's focus on natural empathy was revolutionary.[36]

The 'impartial spectator', Smith's imaginary figure, is used as a type of ethical barometer when humans are faced with situations of moral action. Theft is bad, so we accuse thieves and want them to face prosecution. Social workers dedicate their time to those less fortunate, so we applaud and are inclined to help them. We sympathise with grief but not with greed. It is through social interaction that we learn what is acceptable or not to others. Therefore moral action is not solely a calculated act but also an instinctive response.

Conscience for Smith has a major role in social behaviour. It prevents us from becoming too focused on our own well-being; it forces us to consider the plight of others; it can act as a deterrent when seeking gain at their expense. Conscience is:

> the man within, the great judge and arbiter of our conduct. It is he who, whenever we are about to act in some way that will affect the happiness of others, calls to us with a voice capable of astonishing the most presumptuous of our passions![37]

According to Smith, the truly 'virtuous person' has three key attributes: prudence, justice and beneficence. Prudence prevents excess. Justice ensures ill-behaviour is punished, thus preventing it. Beneficence turns to the well-being of others and subsequently improves societal norms as a whole.[38] Why does he place prudence first, and how does prudence impact on one's life and, indeed, one's approach to saving?

In broad terms, prudence in life is essential because without any form of self-restraint all else falls apart. As Professor Michael Brady argues:

> Without prudent conduct and behavior at the individual level, nothing else is possible. Prudence is the bedrock foundation upon which all other virtues are built. There can be no successful display of courage, temperance, self-command, justice, beneficence, benevolence, charity, concern for others or the interests of others, without prudence having been practiced successfully first.[39]

When it comes to saving, prudence is not a limiter but an enabler. It allows the individual or household to build savings. A degree of self-restraint is not, as it may superficially appear, a hindrance to achieving a given objective. Rather it advances the given objective by limiting the dangers that may arise from human misjudgement, impulsiveness and excess – which can take the form of surplus or scarcity.

As Smith writes: 'prudence is opposed to exposing our health, fortune, rank, or our reputation to any sort of risk.'[40] It maintains a sense of caution about our current situation and surroundings. It works to preserve any benefits we enjoy and protect them for the future. It is reluctant to exchange present certainty for greater future promises. Prudence is, in essence, a basic human virtue in building solid, long-lasting foundations.

Smith rightly argues that prudence is beneficial for building both material *and* social foundations: 'The prudent man is always sincere. He hates the thought of exposing himself to the disgrace that comes from the detection of falsehood.'[41] The prudent person is reliable and therefore trustworthy – and trustworthiness is one of the main social benchmarks that can affect someone's long-term material stability.

Yet for Smith, the prudent person is not just someone of sincerity but someone who is also a frugal worker, who will sacrifice 'the ease and enjoyment of the present moment for the probable expectation of greater ease and enjoyment later on and for a longer time'.[42]

The same principle also applies to the prudent person's attitude to accumulating financial reserves. As he or she gradually becomes more financially stable, the level of frugality is relaxed in line with growing reserves. New luxuries are modestly enjoyed and comparisons made with times past when they represented the unattainable. Prudence in saving promotes not only the accumulation of savings in the material sense but also the principle of saving from a behavioural perspective. The prudent person is therefore able to enjoy both the emotional comfort that comes with financial stability as well as the new material opportunities – which can affect the individual or, indeed, generate positive change for others.

If we are serious about promoting a culture of saving within a consumerist environment, Adam Smith's emphasis on prudence as the foremost human virtue for creating a good society is advice we ought to heed.

Prudence in Judeo-Christian thought

Prudence assumes great importance within the Judeo-Christian tradition. St Thomas Aquinas ranked it as the first cardinal virtue because of its concern with the intellect.[43] Yet something that makes prudence special is that it does not just rely on rational, intellectual judgement but also on morality – it is both a moral and an intellectual virtue. Prudence is concerned with action and an orderly outcome – with 'the rightly ordered action toward the good ... Prudence regards the doing of an action in the most perfect way.'[44] Within *Summa Theologiae*, Aquinas argues that since prudence is best understood as a virtue that implies the 'rectitude of the appetite', it is therefore the principal or cardinal virtue. Prudence is '*auriga virtutum* (the charioteer of the virtues); it guides the other virtues by setting rule and measure'.[45] Prudence is 'right reason in action'.[46]

Action without prudence risks being foolish and ineffective. The *Catholic Encyclopaedia* points out that 'without prudence bravery becomes foolhardiness; mercy sinks into weakness, and temperance into fanaticism.'[47] Yet prudence must not be confounded with timidity or cowardice – it doesn't restrict but rather enables.

> **'Prudence is concerned with action and an orderly outcome'**

Saint Augustine spoke highly of the four cardinal virtues of prudence, justice, fortitude and temperance. For him, prudence is 'love distinguishing with sagacity between what hinders it and what helps it'.[48] The core for Augustine is love within a Christian understanding, and therefore prudence represents a form of calculated or careful love. Again, this does not seek to limit love but rather increase its effectiveness, thus amplifying it.

The thread of prudence as a virtue is present throughout Scripture. We see it in the wisdom literature of the Old Testament, in the Gospels but also in parts of the Pauline epistles. Proverbs 8.12 introduces prudence as an important counterpart to wisdom: 'I, wisdom, dwell together with prudence; I possess knowledge and discretion' (or as the English Revised Version put it: 'I wisdom have made subtilty my dwelling, and find out knowledge and discretion').

The book of Proverbs consists of proverbs – or sayings – that are carefully observed conclusions about the world that aim to 'identify basic patterns that operate in life'.[49] Within this context, Proverbs 1—11 are essentially a call to wisdom. Yet the fascinating fact is that wisdom is calling to *us*. Personified by a woman's plea, wisdom is calling us to seek her and commit ourselves to discovering the 'ways of God in the world'.[50] Wisdom knows no barriers of race, class or gender.

In Proverbs 8.12 we learn that wisdom comes – or 'dwells' – with prudence, knowledge and discretion. Again, prudence here represents the intellect within a unique dance between morality and intelligence. Morality is driven by faith and intelligence by reason. Professor David Atkinson argues that 'Proverbs here is indicating that our moral development goes hand in hand with our cognitive development: the moral life and the intellectual life should be inseparable in "the fear of the Lord".'[51]

In attaining wisdom, therefore, prudence represents the marriage between good, noble intentions and reason. The English Revised Version called it 'subtilty', the Christian Standard Bible has 'shrewd-ness' – though this often carries negative connotations of ruthlessness or selfishness. But the mistake here is seeing shrewdness in isolation: Proverbs 8.12 portrays it together or in association with 'knowledge and discretion'. Shrewdness becomes effectiveness when it is driven by morality. The New Living Translation perhaps more appropriately translates it 'good judgement'.

Scripture places prudence as a key component in attaining wisdom and developing a Godly character. We see its importance reinstated in Proverbs 14.15: 'The simple believe anything, but the prudent give thought to their steps.' Or as the New American Standard Bible (NASB) puts it: 'The naive believes everything, But the sensible man considers his steps.' Prudence represents yet again a form of calculated intent; it is 'sensibility' in action.

The opposite of prudence is foolishness. The foolish man 'rashly commits himself to things without sufficient knowledge of what is involved or the limits to his own abilities and resources'.[52] Proverbs makes it clear that despite any good intentions, a lack of prudence will lead to poor outcomes. Sensibility, thought and reflection are bearers of clarity and sound judgement.

In Jesus' life we see an exceptional model of both drive and prudence. Indeed, it is reasonable to assume that even before starting his ministry at the age of 30, Jesus had to demonstrate great prudence and awareness as a carpenter. He most likely had to plan, design and estimate costs with Joseph and their customers – his family were in effect small business owners.

'A lack of prudence will lead to poor outcomes'

The remarkable thing is that we see Jesus' prudence applied in many of the parables. In explaining the heavenly kingdom he used principles of human morality to, at least in part, further people's understanding of the divine. We see in Luke 14.28 how he urges his audience to calculate the cost of following him carefully: 'Suppose one of you wants to build a tower. Won't you first sit down and estimate the cost to see if you have enough money to complete it?' Equally (v. 31), he talks about the discrepancy in battle between two uneven armies: 'Or suppose a king is about to go to war against another king. Won't he first sit down and consider whether he is able with ten thousand men to oppose the one coming against him with twenty thousand?'

Jesus' demonstration of prudence was also present at times in his behaviour. In Matthew 12.14–16 we read that:

> the Pharisees went out and plotted how they might kill Jesus. Aware of this, Jesus withdrew from that place. A large crowd followed him, and he healed all who were ill. He warned them not to tell others about him.

Again, behaving prudently did not show a lack of courage; on the contrary, it made the goal of ministering and healing more effective. He 'healed all who were ill [and] warned them not to tell others'. Jesus knew his time to face the cross had not yet come and therefore displayed a remarkable level of discernment throughout his earthly work. Professor R. T. France argues that these verses demonstrate 'Jesus' mastery of the situation, despite his non-aggressive attitude'.[53]

There is a continuing thread of prudent moral teaching within Protestant theology. We see this particularly in John Calvin's work on the moral responsibility of providing for self and family – very much in opposition to consumerism. This is viewed through a framework of self-denial and obedience to God. In *Institutes of the Christian Religion*, Calvin argues that:

> For when Scripture enjoins us to lay aside private regard to ourselves, it not only divests our minds of an excessive longing for wealth, power, or human favour, but also eradicates all ambition and thirst for worldly glory and other more secret pests.[54]

His doctrine of self-denial permeates all aspects of life, including the responsibility to give oneself up in the service of God and others. For Calvin, prudence is therefore intrinsic to leading a Christ-centred life.

In summary, Judeo-Christian teaching values the virtue of prudence most highly. It represents a key element of attaining wisdom as it is portrayed in the Scriptures. Prudence in the Christian sense can be applied to all aspects of living, including one's financial well-being. Without it, good intention risks becoming foolishness.

When it comes to saving, Christianity makes the case for the responsible use of money, a form of stewardship much akin to the whole creation mandate. It is a moral responsibility aimed at society at large. Our finances and savings must become useful tools and not burdensome worry. The ultimate social challenge is to promote an environment in which the responsible allocation of financial resources empowers individuals and households to flourish – in both the temporal and spiritual spheres.

NOTES TO CHAPTER 2

1   YouTube, 'Thinking With Things: Professor Colin Mayer', 3 April 2018; https://www.youtube.com/watch?v=finUxBeQjq0.
2   'Money', *Lexico*; https://www.lexico.com/en/definition/money.
3   Jack Weatherford, *The History of Money*, New York: Three Rivers Press, 1997, p. 20.
4   Ibid., p. 21.
5   Herodotus, *Histories I*, Hertfordshire: Wordsworth Editions, 1996, p. 94.
6   Weatherford, *History of Money*, pp. 35–6.
7   Ray Dalio, 'How the Economic Machine works: A Template for Understanding what is happening now', March, 2012; https://www.zerohedge.com/sites/default/files/images/user3303/imageroot/2012/09/Dalio.pdf.
8   Adam Smith, *The Wealth of Nations, Book II – Of the Accumulation of Capital, or of Productive and Unproductive Labour*, Bartleby Books, 14 September 2019; https://www.bartleby.com/10/203.html.
9   United Nations Environment Programme, 'Inclusive Wealth Report 2018', 22 November 2019; https://www.unenvironment.org/resources/report/inclusive-wealth-report-2018.
10 Justo L. Gonzalez, *Faith and Wealth: A History of Early Christian Ideas on the Origin, Significance, and Use of Money*, Eugene, OR: Wipf & Stock, 2002 (originally San Francisco, CA: Harper & Row, 1990), pp. 6–7.

11 Ibid.

12 Plato, *The Collected Dialogues of Plato*, Oxford: Oxford University Press, 1986, p. 779.

13 Gonzalez, *Faith and Wealth*, p. 7.

14 The ancient Greek playwright Aristophanes is rather similar. He also used political satire and irony as his preferred means of communication, and like many of his contemporaries ridiculed the cultural trends occurring in Greece – not least the perceived fall of society and its moral compass into an abyss of materialism and consumption. See, for example, his *Assemblywoman*; http://classics.mit.edu/Aristophanes/eccles.html.

15 Seneca, *Letter 14: On the Reasons for Withdrawing from the World*, Wikisource, 25 November 2019; https://en.wikisource.org/wiki/Moral_letters_to_Lucilius/Letter_14.

16 Gonzalez, *Faith and Wealth*, p. 18.

17 World Bank, 'Decline of Global Extreme Poverty continues but has slowed: World Bank', 19 September 2018; https://www.worldbank.org/en/news/press-release/2018/09/19/decline-of-global-extreme-poverty-continues-but-has-slowed-world-bank.

18 Gary Cross, *An All-Consuming Century: Why Commercialism Won in Modern America*, New York: Columbia University Press, 2000, p. 1.

19 Cross, *All-Consuming Century*, p. 2.

20 *Science Daily*, 'Consumerism', 2 December 2019; https://www.sciencedaily.com/terms/consumerism.htm.

21 *Independent Press-Telegram, 'Consumerism Label Urged', 1955*, Newspapers.com; https://www.newspapers.com/newspage/17483626.

22 Bank of England, 'How has Growth changed over Time?', 5 November 2019; https://www.bankofengland.co.uk/knowledgebank/how-has-growth-changed-over-time.

23 Jutta Bolt, Marcel Timmer and Jan Luiten van Zanden, 'GDP Per Capita since 1820', in Jan Luiten van Zanden et al. (eds.), *How Was Life? Global Well-being since 1820*, Paris: OECD Publishing, 2014.

24 Deirdre Nansen McCloskey, *Bourgeois Equality: How Ideas, Not Capital or Institutions, Enriched the World*, Chicago, IL: University of Chicago Press, 2016, pp. 25–6.

25 Bernard Mandeville, 'The Fable of the Bees: Private Vices, Public Benefits', Early Modern Texts, 1732, 15 October 2019; https://www.earlymoderntexts.com/assets/pdfs/mandeville1732_1.pdf.

26 Quoted in Molly Triffin, '9 Reasons you overspend', *Her Money*, 6 September 2018; https://www.hermoney.com/save/budgeting/9-reasons-why-you-overspend.

27 Ibid.

28 *LOOK* 21:14, 9 July 1957, p. 10.

29 Rome Reports, 'Pope on Christmas: Don't allow Consumerism to overshadow the Meaning of the Celebration', 10 December 2012; https://www.youtube.com/watch?v=ZCglD3zzoJc.

30 Rome Reports, 'Pope in Santa Marta: The "Disease of Consumerism" goes against Generosity', 26 November 2018; https://www.romereports.com/en/2018/11/26/pope-in-santa-marta-the-disease-of-consumerism-goes-against-generosity.

31 United Nations Environment Programme, 'Global Resources Outlook 2019: Natural Resources for the Future we want'; https://wedocs.unep.org/handle/20.500.11822/27517.

32 Jon Goss, 'The Magic of the Mall: An Analysis of Form, Function, and Meaning in the Contemporary Retail Built Environment', *Annals of the Association of American Geographers* 83:1 (March 1993), pp. 18–47.

33 Adam Smith Institute, article 'The Theory of Moral Sentiments'; https://www.adamsmith.org/the-theory-of-moral-sentiments.

34 Eamonn Butler, *The Condensed Wealth of Nations and the Incredibly Condensed Theory of Moral Sentiments*, London: Adam Smith Institute, 2011, p. 77.

35 Adam Smith, *The Theory of Moral Sentiments*, Part I, New York: Dover Publications, 2006, p. 9.

36 Butler, *Condensed Wealth of Nations*, p. 79.

37 Ibid.

38 Smith, *Theory of Moral Sentiments*, Part VI, p. 128.

39 Michael Emmett Brady, 'Adam Smith's Prudence (Self Interest-Self Love) was the Bedrock Foundation and Necessary Condition for the Attainment of all other Virtues in the Theory of Moral Sentiments and the Wealth of Nations', 29 March 2018; https://ssrn.com/abstract=3152154.

40 Smith, *Theory of Moral Sentiments*, Part VI, p. 112.

41 Ibid., Part VI, p. 113.

42 Ibid., Part VI, p. 113.

43 Scott P. Richert, 'What Are the 4 Cardinal Virtues?', *Learn Religions*, 3 January 2019; https://www.learnreligions.com/the-cardinal-virtues-542142.

44 Andrew Michael Steele, 'On Prudence According to St. Thomas Aquinas', Trumau, Austria: International Theological Institute, 12 July 2019; https://www.google.co.uk/url?sa=t&rct=j&q=&esrc=s&source=web&cd=&cad=rja&uact=8&ved=2ahUKEwio3pD6hMnrAhWEs3EKHVENA64QFjAAegQIAhAB&url=http%3A%2F%2Fwww.academia.

edu%2F20062509%2FOn_Prudence_According_to_St._Thomas_Aquinas%3
Fauto%3Ddownload&usg=AOvVaw0hJ_wkYQGkCDrs1jIZaDUE.

45 Catechism of the Catholic Church, 'Part Three: Life In Christ', §1806; http://www.vatican.va/archive/ccc_css/archive/catechism/p3s1c1a7.htm.

46 St. Thomas Aquinas, *Summa Theologica*, II-II, 47,2; https://www.newadvent.org/summa/3047.htm#article2.

47 'Prudence', New Advent, 22 July 2019; http://www.newadvent.org/cathen/12517b.htm.

48 Saint Augustine, 'Of the Morals of the Catholic Church/De moribus eccl.', Chapter XV.

49 *Apologetics Study Bible*, Nashville, TN: Holman Bible Publishers, 2007, p. 917.

50 David Atkinson, *The Message of Proverbs*, London: Inter-Varsity Press, 1997, p. 45.

51 Ibid.

52 *Apologetics Study Bible*, Commentary on Proverbs 14.15.

53 R .T. France, *The Gospel of Matthew*, Grand Rapids, MI: Eerdmans, 2007, p. 205.

54 John Calvin, *Self-denial*, in *The Institutes of the Christian Religion*, USA: Chapel Library, 2009, p. 3.

CHAPTER 3

CONCLUSIONS AND POLICY RESPONSES

In view of the prevailing low level of and challenges to saving, and with the ideas of prudence and scriptural wisdom in mind, how might we respond on a policy level?

3.1   MAKING SAVING PAY

Ending low interest rates

Government must strive to create an environment that promotes saving. The record low interest rates presented in Chapter 1 reward spending, not saving. It has therefore become cheaper – and more profitable – to borrow than to save. The Covid-19 lockdown imposed in the UK in March 2020 further worsened the macroeconomic picture for savers. As of April, the Federal Reserve reduced interest rates to a low of 0.25 per cent and the Bank of England to 0.1 per cent.

According to Anna Bowes, co-founder of Savings Champion: 'This new but highly anticipated cut by the Bank of England is a huge blow to savers, bringing the base rate to a record low level.'[1] Savers need to have the confidence that their efforts are worthwhile. It is crucial that any economic recovery includes returning interest rates to higher levels. Moreover, this need not come at the cost of spending: a society in a healthy financial position is one with the capacity to spend and to work collectively

'Saving and spending are not mutually exclusive'

towards long-term economic growth. Saving and spending are not mutually exclusive.

Boosting incentives that promote saving

Chapter 1 showed that neither initiatives such as Help to Save/Help to Buy, nor savings accounts, have resulted in a significant improvement in UK rates of saving. At best they have helped a limited number of people, at worst made it harder to save or get on the housing ladder.

A thorough revision of government initiatives to promote saving is required. More specifically, an evaluation is needed of both the desired outcomes of any initiative and who exactly benefits from it. Money-matching schemes such as Help to Save and some ISAs have the potential to encourage saving, but they must become more attractive and accessible for those who need them most. A good start would be shorter pay-out times and greater clarity on how the funds are being spent by the beneficiaries.

Tax incentives should also play a greater role in encouraging saving. The tax-free Personal Allowance, at its recently relatively high levels, and Personal Savings Allowance are welcome initiatives but require further development to make them more broadly available. Perhaps the Savings Allowance should be expanded for basic-rate taxpayers to match the Personal Allowance.

Equally, ISAs are having limited impact. It is deeply disappointing that since the government launched Lifetime ISAs in 2017, *no* major high street bank has offered them to the public – which has cost many the opportunity to earn the 25 per cent government bonus on savings. Hannah Maundrell, the editor-in-chief of Money.co.uk, attributed banks' failure to adopt LISAs to lack of coordination between policy and industry: 'Yet again the government has promised consumers the chance of a shiny new savings vehicle without consulting with the industry on how and when they can deliver it.'[2] Government has to ensure that such saving initiatives will be adopted by those who actually have to make them available to the public. New initiatives must carry a palatable level of risk as well as financial feasibility before being rolled out. The hope is that greater cooperation between the public and private sector will lead to more widespread adoption of such saving initiatives in future.

3.2 HOME OWNERSHIP AND INTRA-GENERATIONAL EQUITY

Getting on the housing ladder

The lack of affordable homes remains one of the most pressing issues facing the UK. What makes it particularly worrying is that the younger generations are the hardest hit by inflated prices. To put things in perspective, the average home price in 2015–16 was two and a half times that in 1995–6 (adjusted to inflation), while income levels for 25–34-year-olds grew by just a fifth in the same period.[3] As mentioned in Chapter 1, this translates to a home ownership rate of around 24 per cent among 25–34-year-olds, compared to almost 80 per cent for those aged 65 and above.

'The UK needs to build more homes' It is dire that a high-income country such as the UK presents its younger generations with such a prohibitively expensive housing market. After all, it will be they who drive the national economy forward. Achieving home ownership is a key milestone in British life and culture. It confers a sense of safety and stability that, to varying degrees, roots people in local communities and contributes to family life. The reality is that home ownership remains a significant aspiration for young people.

The UK needs to build more homes. Its restrictive planning laws may be causing more harm than good, particularly in areas of low congestion where there is an abundance of space but no permission to build. And this need not come at the expense of green areas, historical sites or nature reserves.

A study by the ONS in 2010 found that only 12 per cent of the UK's land mass is 'developed land', while some 65 per cent is 'agricultural land'.[4] So the data shows that there is plenty of space for homebuilding. Virtually every other sector of the economy allows for supply to meet demand – surely more can be done to achieve this in the case of homebuilding. However, it must be acknowledged that over the last decade or so there have been sporadic signs of improvement. Newbuilds for 2018–19 peaked at just over 240,000, the highest number in over 30 years. The Home Builder's Federation estimates that over 380,000 homes are already in the pipeline but that more political and legislative support is needed to reach the government target of 300,000 newbuilds per year by the mid-2020s.[5] These are all encouraging signs, but unless there is legislative support in relaxing some of the UK's restrictive planning, the apparent success may be short lived. It remains to be seen how the pledged reforms under Boris Johnson's premiership play out.

Pensions and the triple lock

The other much-contended area in the public space is pensions or retirement savings. As touched on in Chapter 1, the expansion and wider availability of private or workplace pensions is a welcome development. The increase in workplace contributions noted by the IFS is likely to have a positive impact on retirement savings for millions in the long run.

Yet more needs to be done in further diversifying the private investment options for households and individuals. The general public needs clarity about what private retirement vehicles are available to them and what the risk levels actually mean. Companies such as Vanguard or HSBC are already offering a portfolio of retirement and index funds in which individuals can invest directly without the use of an intermediary or broker.

The problem, however, remains a lack of awareness and basic investment knowledge. More needs to be done to ensure that people are aware of available saving opportunities. The encouraging news is that this can be achieved either through a campaign by the private sector (with its vested interest in attracting new customers), a government-run campaign or any other public or private measures that would get the message out. Solutions like these are not just achievable but also beneficial to all participants involved: healthier finances for households and individuals; increased customers for financial institutions; greater tax revenues for government.

Changes also need to take place in the state pension. There seems to be a growing consensus that the triple lock cannot continue for much longer in its current format. It was noted in Chapter 1 that it is financially unfeasible to maintain the 2.5 per cent guarantee indefinitely, particularly in times when real-wage growth has been minimal.

The triple lock also does little to assist those who are already on low pensions and therefore rely on pension credit for additional income. In reality it predominantly helps those already financially stable and in no need of extra income. According to Baroness Ros Altmann, Pensions Minister under David Cameron:

> The triple lock made some sense when it was first introduced ... but actually it is a little bit of a trick because it doesn't apply to all state pensioners and in fact it doesn't apply to Pension Credit which is what the poorest pensioners live on – those are

the ones you want to protect. The 2.5 per cent is an illogical arbitrary figure ... effectively it's not got any economic or social rationale.[6]

That is not to say that state pensions should remain stagnant. However, increases should be in line with and not greater than wage earnings. A proposed 'double lock' eliminates the 2.5 per cent figure but ensures that pensions still rise by either inflation or wage growth, whichever is higher. However, research conducted by the IFS found that a double lock may still lead to pensions outstripping wages over time and therefore needs a 'time-barred link between the value of the state pension, earnings and prices'.[7]

'Prudence does not restrict but rather enables'

Revising the triple lock is about fiscal responsibility, not reducing income for pensioners. It is about empowering the young and those in the workforce to build up savings of their own, and about ensuring that taxes are used efficiently. Again, these are not issues that operate in a vacuum. A financially stable workforce contributes to both economic growth as well as tax revenue – this is why the UK would benefit from a revision in public pensions.

3.3   PRUDENCE AND ESTABLISHING A CULTURE OF SAVING

A society in which financial prudence is practised is more likely to steward resources and thus contribute positively to overall economic growth. Chapter 2 looked at the virtue of prudence and how it is essential for developing a habit of saving. Prudence does not restrict but rather enables and empowers. It is not a limiting force but one that guides and harnesses intent and makes it more effective. We have seen how, for Adam Smith, prudence also works to preserve the things we enjoy and protect them for the future. It enhances present certainty and future promises; it is a fundamental human virtue in building robust, long-lasting foundations.

But can prudence be embodied in policy? The National Savings Movement that operated for most of the twentieth century is an intriguing case of mass mobilisation to promote saving across the UK. This is not to say it demonstrated the embodiment of prudence per se, but it recognised that prudent, continuous saving is a national practice to be cherished.

At its peak in the 1950s the Movement had over 7 million subscribers and £6 billion in savings (£2.1 trillion adjusted to inflation).[8] Alongside saving itself, another notable achievement was providing funding for the war effort in the 1940s. The War Office issued government bonds that were bought through the Movement. Banners and posters encouraged contribution with messages such as: 'Keep On Saving – Salute The Soldier'; 'Britain's Sea Power – Maintain it With Your Savings'; 'The Most You Can Save is the Least They Deserve'.[9] While this is not necessarily an argument that the UK should re-establish the Movement in the historical sense, it should re-establish the public recognition that saving and savings are indeed essential to the well-being of society. The National Savings Movement served the twentieth century; now a renewed emphasis with the same ethos is needed for the twenty-first.

Financial education in schools

We need to reassess what school is for. Surely it is to prepare children for life, in which case helping them manage money is just as important as imparting knowledge of science, English literature or history. We should reassess the purpose of education and its effectiveness in equipping future generations.

One proposal is the introduction of basic financial education in schools and the National Curriculum. This is a desirable and achievable objective that would probably command support across the political spectrum. It bears no political colour or ideology and the long-term impact – however large or small – is only likely to be positive. It also has the potential to prevent millions of children ending up in damaging financial situations later in life. Basic financial education is not something policymakers can afford to ignore.

It is, however, important to emphasise the 'basic': the aim is not to teach children advanced financial concepts but to equip them with an elementary understanding of budgeting, pensions, credit and savings.

Ideally this could be placed on GCSE and/or A-Level curricula, the reason being that for many, university or apprenticeship programmes will be the first time they have independence over a credit or debit card. And for some it will be the first time they have had to live within a budget. So giving pupils the chance to learn about money and budgeting – and then the perfect opportunity to put theory into practice – could be a highly effective educational tool.

Some may argue that teachers are already stretched and there is no more room in the curricula for adding new subjects. In some schools this may be the case, but financial education doesn't need to be an individual subject – it could become a new focus for oft-criticised curriculum areas such as Citizenship.

Another objection may be that financial education is the responsibility of parents. Again, while true to some extent, in many cases parents themselves have little grasp of financial matters; and even those who do may not have the time or inclination to discuss them with their children.

The good news is that some schools have already taken the initiative themselves and offer students basic financial education. However, they are severely lacking in direction and support. Research conducted by the Money Advice Service found that while 92 per cent of schools in England believe it is part of their role to provide financial education, and 72 per cent would like to increase provision, only 59 per cent feel they have the necessary knowledge and skills.[10] This might also be an area in which the development of links with local businesses and business leaders would be fruitful.

Now is an opportune time to give schools the support they are asking for and protect younger generations from avoidable stumbling blocks later in life.

Innovation and a more active role for business

Companies that have a closer relationship with employees are in a better position to help promote saving. Government needs to do its part and support businesses that actively seek to care for the financial well-being of their people. For instance, it could help them grow by increasing their access to additional capital. A report conducted by the Centre for Policy Studies found that SMEs in the UK are far too reliant on banks for debt financing. The opening of a retail bond market – as in the USA – could potentially close an estimated £35 billion funding gap for SMEs.[11] The outcomes would be not just more but also better-paid jobs, as well as an increase in disposable income for households across the country – and a growing economy is essential for encouraging a culture of saving.

'Financial knowledge will impact all facets of society'

Encouraging companies to think how they might promote saving among their employees is just as much an ethical approach to business as corporate governance codes or rewriting articles of association.

Technology and financial awareness

Technology's impact on finances cannot be overstated. Beyond the gradual disappearance of cash considered in the Introduction lie the associated difficulties and confusion of an increasingly complex spending system. From credit-card points to cryptocurrency, the lines between what we have as traditional 'money' in the bank and what we can spend have been blurred. Within such a context, financial literacy becomes crucial if people are to avoid the pitfalls of cash versus credit.

While a more thorough review of the effect of technology is required, the importance is universal: lack of both financial and technical knowledge will impact all facets of society. A plethora of causes are being fought in the public sphere, from climate change to mental health – saving and financial awareness should join them.

NOTES TO CHAPTER 3

1   Stephanie Spicer, 'Interest Rate Cuts bad for Savers and Little for Investors', *What Investment*, 20 March 2020; https://www.whatinvestment.co.uk/interest-rate-cuts-bad-for-savers-and-little-for-investors-2617482.
2   'Banks and Building Societies snub Lifetime Isa Launch', *BBC News*, 6 April 2017; https://www.bbc.co.uk/news/business-39506199.
3   Ben Chapman, 'Home Ownership falls more in UK than any other EU Country', *The Independent*, 21 August 2018; https://www.independent.co.uk/news/business/analysis-and-features/uk-home-ownership-falls-more-than-eu-country-france-poland-property-market-a8501836.html.
4   Jawed Khan and Tamara Powell, 'Land Use in the UK', Office for National Statistics, 2010.
5   Hilary Osborne, 'Housebuilding in England at 30-year High, Government Data shows', *The Guardian*, 14 November 2019; https://www.theguardian.com/society/2019/nov/14/house-building-in-england-at-30-year-high-government-data-show.

6   YouTube, 'BBC Newsnight Interview', 2 May 2017; https://www.youtube.com/watch?v=C9wqVEmB6ww.

7   Charles Walmsley, 'IFS: Even "Double Lock" on State Pension is Bad Idea', *Citywire*, 28 April 2017; https://citywire.co.uk/funds-insider/news/ifs-even-double-lock-on-state-pension-is-bad-idea/a1012254.

8   'National Savings Movement: Oral Answers to Questions – National Finance – in the House of Commons at 12:00 am on 21st November 1950', *They Work for You*; https://www.theyworkforyou.com/debates/?id=1950-11-21a.203.6.

9   Imperial War Museum, 'Historical Archive of Posters', 8 November 2019; https://www.iwm.org.uk/collections/search?filters per cent5BtermString per cent5D per cent5Bwar per cent20loans per cent20 per cent2F per cent20savings per cent5D=on.

10 'Financial Education in Secondary Schools in England', Money Advice Service, November 2018.

11 Rishi Sunak MP, 'A New Era for Retail Bonds', Centre for Policy Studies, 15 November 2017; https://www.cps.org.uk/research/a-new-era-for-retail-bonds.

Sources for figures and tables

Figure 1.1:   *Office for National Statistics*

Figure 1.2:   *Institute for Fiscal Studies, Living standards, poverty and inequality in the UK: 2018, 20 June 2018*

Figure 1.3:   *Office for National Statistics, Labour productivity time series, 6 July 2018; Office for Budget Responsibility, Economical and fiscal outlook March 2018, 13 March 2018; and Treasury Committee staff calculations*

Figure 1.4:   *House of Commons Treasury Committee*

Figure 1.5:   *Trading Economics/Bank of England*

Figure 1.6:   *bogleheads.org*

Figure 1.7:   *Interactive Investor*

Figure 1.8:   *Trading Economics/US Bureau of Economic Analysis*

Figure 1.9:   *US Federal Reserve (Survey of Consumer Finances), sourced from Haver Analytics; Deloitte Services LP economic analysis*

Table 1.1:   *Office for National Statistics*

COMPLETE LIST OF CEME PUBLICATIONS

Richard Turnbull, *Quaker Capitalism: Lessons for Today*, 2014.

Edward Carter, *God and Enterprise*, 2016.

Richard Turnbull (ed.), *The Challenge of Social Welfare: Seeking a New Consensus*, 2016.

Richard Turnbull, *The Moral Case for Asset Management (jointly with New City Initiative)*, 2016.

Martin Schlag, *Business in Catholic Social Thought*, 2016.

Andrei Rogobete, *Ethics in Global Business*, 2016.

Ben Cooper, *The Economics of the Hebrew Scriptures*, 2017.

Lyndon Drake, *Capital Markets for the Good of Society*, 2017.

Richard Turnbull and Tim Weinhold (eds), *Making Capitalism Work for Everyone, Vol. 1*, 2017.

Richard Turnbull and Tim Weinhold (eds), *Making Capitalism Work for Everyone, Vol. 2*, 2017.

Richard Turnbull, *Understanding the Common Good*, 2017.

Andrei Rogobete, *The Challenges of Migration*, 2018.

Steven Morris, *Enterprise and Entrepreneurship: Doing Good Through the Local Church*, 2018.

Richard Turnbull, *Work as Enterprise: Recovering a Theology of Work*, 2019.

Edward Carter, *God and Competition: Towards a Positive Theology of Competitive Behaviour*, 2019.

Steven Morris, *The Business of God*, 2019.

Andrew Hartropp, *Corporate Executive Remuneration*, 2019.

Richard Turnbull (ed.), *The Economic and Social Teaching of the Hebrew Scriptures*, 2020.

Andrei Rogobete, *The UK Savings Crisis*, 2020.